UK Air Fryer

Cookbook For Beginners

1900 Days Super-easy ,Crispy and Affordable Homemade
Air Fryer Recipes for Smart People to Cook Faster and
Healthier (2023 Edition)

Donna D. Batista

Contents

Introduction

As a young professional in my mid-twenties, I am always on the lookout for convenient and healthy ways to cook my meals. One busy Saturday afternoon, while browsing the kitchen appliances section of a home goods store, I stumbled upon a sleek stainless-steel air fryer that caught my eye. Intrigued by the promise of crispy and delicious fried foods with little to no oil, I struck up a conversation with a store associate who happened to be a self-proclaimed air fryer enthusiast.

To my surprise, the store associate was a male, challenging the stereotype that women are expected to be knowledgeable about kitchen appliances. He enthusiastically explained the benefits of air frying, from healthier cooking options to versatility in preparing a wide range of dishes. His passion and knowledge were contagious, and I found myself drawn to the air fryer even more.

After much contemplation, I decided to take the plunge and purchase the air fryer. I eagerly took it home and wasted no time in experimenting with it. I tried making crispy fries, juicy chicken wings, and even a batch of homemade doughnuts. With each successful attempt, my excitement grew, and I became more confident in my culinary skills.

One day, I decided to host a dinner party for my closest friends. I invited friends from diverse backgrounds, each with their own dietary preferences. I wanted to showcase the versatility of the air fryer and cater to different tastes. I prepared a feast of air-fried appetizers, main courses, and even dessert. My friends were amazed by the incredible flavors and textures of the food, and their genuine admiration for my culinary skills was heartwarming. It challenged the stereotype that women's cooking is often taken for granted and highlighted my talent and hard work in the kitchen.

Inspired by my air frying adventures, I decided to start a food blog. I wanted to share my love for cooking, air frying, and inspire others to try new recipes and cooking methods. Through my blog, I aimed to challenge traditional gender roles and

showcase empowered female characters who pursue their passions with confidence and success. Starting the food blog ignited my entrepreneurial spirit and creativity. I poured my heart and soul into creating content, experimenting with new recipes, and sharing my air frying adventures. My blog gained a following, and I was thrilled to connect with like-minded food enthusiasts who appreciated my culinary skills and innovative approach to cooking.

My fateful encounter with the air fryer opened up a world of possibilities in the kitchen and transformed my love for cooking. It empowered me to challenge stereotypes, pursue my passions, and share my culinary journey with others. I will forever be grateful for that chance encounter and the incredible meals that it brought into my life.

How Exactly Do Air Fryers Cook Food?

Air fryers have gained significant popularity as a modern kitchen appliance that offers a healthier alternative to traditional deep frying. At the heart of an air fryer's cooking mechanism is convection cooking, which utilises hot air circulation to achieve crispy and evenly cooked results.

Within the air fryer, a high-powered fan circulates hot air at high velocities, creating a vortex of heat. The food is typically placed in a basket or on a tray, allowing the hot air to surround it from all angles. The hot air rapidly evaporates the surface moisture of the food, resulting in a crispy texture reminiscent of deep frying.

For example, when making homemade sweet potato fries, the hot air in the air fryer quickly evaporates the moisture on the surface of the fries, creating a crispy exterior while keeping the interior tender. Similarly, when air frying chicken tenders, the hot air circulates around the tender pieces, creating a golden-brown crust without the need for excess oil.

I have personally experimented with various foods in my air fryer, including fish fillets, vegetables like Brussels sprouts and asparagus, and even homemade onion rings. The results have been

consistently impressive, with perfectly crispy and evenly cooked outcomes. The speed and convenience of cooking with an air fryer have made it a versatile and practical addition to my kitchen, allowing me to enjoy a wide range of fried foods with reduced oil content and minimal mess to clean up.

In conclusion, air fryers utilise the convection cooking method, where hot air circulation creates a crispy texture on food with minimal oil usage. The precise and consistent cooking results make air fryers a popular choice for health-conscious individuals who enjoy the taste and texture of fried foods without the excess oil.

What Kinds of Foods Can You Cooked in An Air Fryer?

A question that beginners usually ask is, "What can I cook in my air fryer?" The answer is that there are countless possibilities. From flavorful chicken wings and juicy steaks to flaky fish and golden-brown onion rings, air fryers are versatile and can handle a variety of dishes. With a bit of experimentation, you can discover your favorite air fryer recipes and enjoy healthy and delicious meals.

Here are eight nutritious and scrumptious foods to cook in an air fryer:

Chicken: Air fried chicken is juicy on the inside and crispy on the outside, with less oil than traditional fried chicken.

Fish: Air frying fish creates a perfectly crispy exterior and a moist, flaky interior, without any greasy residue.

Vegetables: Air frying vegetables such as Brussels sprouts, cauliflower, and broccoli is an excellent method to make them crispy and caramelized while preserving their nutritional value.

French fries: Air fried French fries are crispy on the outside and soft on the inside, with less oil and fewer calories than deep-fried versions.

Bacon: Air frying bacon results in perfectly crispy bacon without the mess of grease splatters.

Donuts: Air frying donuts creates a crispy exterior and a soft, fluffy interior without the need for deep frying.

Tofu: Air frying tofu creates a crispy exterior and a tender interior, making it a great plant-based protein option.

Baked goods: Air fryers can also be used to bake a variety of desserts such as muffins, cakes, and brownies with less fat and fewer calories than traditional baking methods.

These are just a few examples of the many delicious and healthy foods you can cook in an air fryer. With a bit of creativity, you can air fry almost anything and enjoy the same delicious outcomes with fewer calories and less fat.

What to Avoid in An Air Fryer

In this article, I will be discussing the six types of foods that you should not cook in an air fryer to avoid danger.

Batter-Coated Foods: Foods that are coated in batter, such as fish or chicken, should be avoided in an air fryer. The hot air circulating in the fryer will make the batter to fly off and potentially cause a fire hazard.

Liquid-Based Batters: Foods that require a liquid-based batter, such as onion rings or tempura, should also be avoided. The circulating air will cause the batter to be blown off, resulting in uneven cooking and potential mess.

Overfilled Foods: It is important to not overfill the air fryer basket as this can result in uneven cooking or even cause the fryer to malfunction. Ensure that there is sufficient space between the pieces of food.

High-Fat Foods: Avoid cooking high-fat foods such as bacon or sausages in an air fryer. The excess fat will cause smoke and potential fire hazards.

Raw Vegetables: Raw vegetables such as broccoli

or carrots may not cook evenly in an air fryer. It is best to pre-cook them before placing them in the fryer to ensure that they are cooked uniformly.

Small Foods: Small, loose foods such as peas or popcorn should not be cooked in an air fryer. The circulating air can blow these small pieces around and potentially cause burns or even damage the fryer.

In conclusion, it is important to remember that not all foods are suitable to be cooked in an air fryer. When using this kitchen appliance, ensure that the foods are appropriate for the fryer, and follow the manufacturer's instructions carefully to avoid potential danger.

Why You Should Consider Owning One?

Are you tired of spending hours in the kitchen preparing meals that aren't as healthy or tasty as you'd like them to be? Have you been looking for a cooking appliance that will help you save time and reduce the mess when preparing your favourite foods? If so, now is the time to consider owning an air fryer.

·Healthy Gourmet

Air frying uses hot air to cook food without oil or with as little oil as possible, making it a healthier alternative to deep frying. This means you can enjoy crispy, tasty food without the added calories and unhealthy fats.

· Time-saving

Air fryers are an incredibly efficient way to cook food quickly. They preheat in just a few minutes, and most foods cook in less than 20 minutes. This makes them perfect for those who are short on time but still want to enjoy a home-cooked meal.

·User Friendly

Air fryers are incredibly user-friendly. Simply set the temperature and cooking time, and the appliance will do the rest. They require minimal monitoring, and most models have a built-in timer and automatic shut-off feature.

·Versatile Cooking:

Air fryers can be used to cook a wide variety of foods, including chicken, fish, vegetables, and even desserts. With its ability to cook food evenly, you can enjoy perfectly roasted carrots, crispy broccoli, and tender chicken, all in one appliance.

·Less Mess

Unlike traditional deep frying, air fryers don't require a large amount of oil, meaning there is less mess to clean up. Additionally, most air fryer baskets and trays are dishwasher safe, making clean-up a breeze.

·Energy Efficient

Efficiency is always at the forefront of our minds these days with the cost of living crisis making any electrical appliances a little nerve-wracking to use. Air fryers use significantly less energy than traditional ovens and deep fryers, making them an eco-friendly option.

·Compact and space-saving

Air Fryers are relatively small, and many models are designed to fit on your kitchen countertop, making them a space-saving option for small kitchens.

How to Clean Your Air Fryer?

One of the most innovative appliances that has come onto the market in recent years is the air fryer. Its ability to fry food with little to no oil while maintaining a crispy, golden-brown texture has made it a popular addition to many kitchens.

For those who are just starting out with an air fryer, cleaning an unfamiliar appliance can be a little intimidating. But with a few simple tips and tricks, you can master the use and maintenance of your new fryer.

Firstly, it is important to preheat your air fryer before use. This ensures that your food is cooked evenly and at the correct temperature. Most air fryers have a preheat setting that you can use. Simply turn on the air fryer and choose the preheat setting, and allow it to heat up for a few minutes.

Next, you should keep in mind that you may need to adjust the cooking time and temperature for different types of food. It is always a good idea to refer to your air fryer's user manual for suggested cooking times and temperatures. However, as a general rule, you can use a lower temperature and shorter cooking time than you would with a traditional oven. The above steps so far will significantly reduce your later effort on cleaning.

When it comes to cleaning your air fryer, it is important to do so regularly to keep it in good condition. You should always let the appliance cool down completely before cleaning it. Then, you can remove the basket and any other removable parts and wash them in warm, soapy water.

To clean the inside of the air fryer, you can use a soft-bristled brush or cloth to gently wipe away any food residue. If there are any stubborn stains or burnt-on food, you can use a mixture of baking soda and water to create a paste and spread it over the affected area. Allow it to sit for a few minutes before wiping it away with a damp cloth.

The air fryer can be a versatile and practical addition to any kitchen. With a little patience and practice, you can become a pro at using and maintaining your air fryer. Always remember to preheat the appliance, adjust cooking times and temperatures as needed, and keep it clean to ensure longevity.

Anything to Avoid When Using an Air Fryer ?

If you're new to using an air fryer, there are a few things to consider before diving in. First and foremost, it's important to understand what types of food are well-suited for air frying. Some of my personal favorites include chicken wings, sweet potato fries, and even desserts like apple turnovers

or mini cheesecakes.

However, there are a few foods that I would recommend avoiding when using an air fryer. For example, anything with a wet batter or coating (such as tempura shrimp or fried chicken) may not turn out as crispy as you would like. Additionally, delicate items like fish or thin-cut vegetables can cook too quickly and become overdone if you're not careful.

When it comes to preparing your food for air frying, there are a few tips and tricks to keep in mind. First, make sure to pat dry any ingredients that are naturally moist (such as chicken or tofu) before seasoning and adding to the basket. This will help prevent sogginess and ensure a crispy finish.

Another important factor is the temperature and cook time. Every air fryer is slightly different, so it may take a bit of trial and error to find the perfect settings for your favorite recipes. As a general rule of thumb, I recommend starting with a lower temperature (around 350°F) and checking on your food regularly to ensure its cooking evenly.

Lastly, don't be afraid to get creative with your air fryer. This appliance is incredibly versatile and can be used to cook everything from roasted vegetables to homemade granola. So, grab your favorite cookbook or food blog, and start exploring all the possibilities!

Air Fryer Safety Concerns

Check the basket and tray regularly
Make sure to inspect the basket and tray regularly for any signs of wear or damage. If there are any cracks or chips, replace the affected parts as soon as possible to avoid affecting the quality of your food.

Preheating The Air Fryer

It's important to preheat your air fryer before you begin cooking. Doing so will get the oil or grease inside the appliance up to the right temperature, which will make for more consistent temperatures and faster cooking time.

Do not overload

Essentially, an Air Fryer is a small oven. Cooking with it, sometimes when you are cooking chicken breasts in the regular oven, means you will be forced to stack the food on top of each other. With this scenario, you will force to overload the basket, which is unsuitable for the Fryer.

Avoid Using a Dirty Air Fryer

Cleaning your air fryer should be frequent, that is, after every use or after some uses. That will ensure your air fryer works efficiently in your cooking process.Moreover, cleaning the fryer from the inside doesn't take long; all you need is 5 minutes at most!

Avoid metal utensils

When cooking with your Air Fryer, it's best to avoid using metal utensils, as these can scratch the basket and cause food to stick. Instead, use plastic, silicone, or wood utensils.

Don't use aluminum foil

The primary purpose of air fryers is to cook meals without excessive oil. Air fryers are a blessing for people who want to enjoy crispy food without too much oil. Some recipes may require a tiny amount of oil to prepare a delicious meal. Therefore, add only the amount asked and avoid adding a lot of oil as it may cause a fire.

Unplug the cord after use

Keeping an appliance plugged in after use can lead to accidents. It is therefore important to unplug electrical appliances immediately after use to avoid any dangerous situations.

With these care tips, you'll be equipped to clean and maintain your air fryer .Hopefully you can borrow this book as a springboard to avoid these common mistakes.

Chapter 1 Breakfast Recipes

Air Fryer Bacon and Egg Breakfast Sandwich Recipe

Prep time: 5 minutes

Cooking Time: 20 minutes

Serves: 4 sandwiches

Ingredients
- 8 slices of bacon
- 4 large eggs
- 1 tablespoon milk
- Salt and pepper, to taste
- 4 English muffins, sliced in half
- 4 slices of cheese

Preparation Instructions
1. Preheat the air fryer to 400°F (200°C).
2. Place the bacon slices in a single layer in the air fryer basket. Make sure you spray the air fryer basket with a non stick cooking spray or use a purpose made air fryer liner.
3. Cook the bacon for 7-10 minutes, or until crispy. Add an extra minute or two if you like your bacon extra crispy!
4. Remove the bacon from the air fryer and place it on a paper towel to drain. Pat the excess fat off of the bacon with an extra paper towel.
5. In a bowl, whisk together the eggs, milk, salt, and pepper.
6. Pour the egg mixture into the air fryer basket and cook for 5-7 minutes, or until fully cooked.
7. Toast the English muffins in the air fryer for 2-3 minutes, or until golden brown.
8. Assemble the sandwich by placing a slice of cheese on each toasted muffin, followed by a slice of bacon and a portion of the scrambled eggs.
9. Serve immediately and enjoy!

Air Fryer Glazed Bacon Recipe

Prep time: 5 minutes

Cooking Time: 10 minutes

Serves: 2 people

Ingredients
- 8 slices of bacon
- 2 tablespoons brown sugar
- 1 tablespoon maple syrup
- 1 teaspoon Dijon mustard
- Salt and pepper, to taste

Preparation Instructions
1. Preheat the air fryer to 400°F (200°C).
2. In a small bowl, mix together the brown sugar, maple syrup, Dijon mustard, salt, and pepper to create the glaze.
3. Place the bacon slices in a single layer in the air fryer basket. Spray the basket with a non stick cooking spray or use a specific air fryer liner to prevent the bacon from sticking to the basket.
4. Brush the glaze evenly over the bacon slices. For this step you can use a pastry brush or a silicon glazing brush.
5. Cook the bacon for 7-10 minutes, or until crispy and glaze has caramelised. For extra crispy bacon you can add an extra minute or two to the Cooking Time.
6. Remove the bacon from the air fryer and place it on a paper towel to drain. Pat the top of the bacon dry with another paper towel.
7. Serve immediately and enjoy!

Air Fryer Breakfast Tostadas Recipe

Prep time: 5 minutes

Cooking Time: 10-15 minutes

Serves: 4 people

Ingredients
- 4 corn tortillas
- 300 g black beans, drained and rinsed
- 300 g shredded cheddar cheese
- 4 large eggs
- Salt and pepper, to taste
- Salsa, avocado, hot sauce, and cilantro, for serving (optional)

Preparation Instructions
1. Preheat the air fryer to 400°F (200°C).
2. Place the tortillas in a single layer in the air fryer basket. Then you can spray them with a butter flavoured cooking spray.
3. Cook the tortillas for 2-3 minutes, or until crispy and lightly golden.
4. Remove the tortillas from the air fryer and set aside.
5. In a bowl, mash the black beans with a fork.
6. Spread a layer of mashed black beans on each tortilla, followed by a sprinkle of shredded cheese.
7. In another bowl, whisk together the eggs, salt, and pepper.
8. Pour the egg mixture into the air fryer basket and cook for 5-7 minutes, or until fully cooked.
9. Place the cooked eggs on top of the cheese and black beans on each tortilla.
10. Return the tostadas to the air fryer and cook for an additional 2-3 minutes, or until the cheese is melted.
11. Serve the tostadas immediately with salsa, avocado, hot sauce, and cilantro, if desired.
12. Enjoy this tasty and easy air fryer breakfast tostada recipe!

Air Fryer Soft Pretzels

Prep time: 20 minutes

Cook Time: 10 minutes

Serves: 4

Ingredients
- 1 ½ cups (180g) all-purpose flour
- 1 tbsp (12g) sugar
- ½ tsp (3g) salt
- 1 tsp (4g) instant yeast
- ½ cup (120ml) warm water
- 1 tbsp (15ml) vegetable oil
- ¼ cup (60g) baking soda
- 1 egg yolk, beaten
- Coarse salt for sprinkling

Preparation Instructions
1. In a mixing bowl, combine the flour, sugar, salt, and instant yeast.
2. Add the warm water and vegetable oil, and stir until a dough forms.
3. Knead the dough on a floured surface until it becomes smooth and elastic, for about 5-7 minutes.
4. Divide the dough into 4 equal pieces and roll each piece into a long rope.
5. Shape each rope into a pretzel shape.
6. Preheat your air fryer to 190°C.
7. In a saucepan, bring 2 cups (480ml) of water to a boil and add the baking soda.
8. Carefully place each pretzel into the boiling water for 30 seconds.
9. Remove the pretzels from the water with a slotted spoon and place them on a paper towel to drain.
10. Brush the beaten egg yolk over the pretzels and sprinkle with coarse salt.
11. Place the pretzels in the air fryer basket and cook for 10 minutes or until golden brown and crispy.
12. Once the pretzels are done, remove them

from the air fryer and serve immediately.

Air Fryer Bagels

Prep time: 15 minutes

Cook Time: 10 minutes

Serves: 4

Ingredients
- 1 ½ cups (187. 5g) all-purpose flour
- 2 tsp (9. 9g) granulated sugar
- 1 ½ tsp (7. 4g) instant yeast
- ¾ tsp (3. 7g) salt
- 2/3 cup (158. 7ml) warm water
- 1 egg white
- 1 tbsp (14. 8ml) water
- Sesame seeds, poppy seeds, or everything bagel seasoning, for topping

Preparation Instructions
1. In a large mixing bowl, combine the flour, sugar, yeast, and salt. Add in the warm water and mix until a dough forms.
2. Knead the dough for 5-7 minutes or until it becomes smooth and elastic.
3. Divide the dough into 4 equal parts and shape each one into a ball. Flatten each ball slightly and make a hole in the center using your finger.
4. Preheat your air fryer to 180°C.
5. In a small bowl, whisk together the egg white and water. Brush the mixture over the top of the bagels.
6. Sprinkle the toppings of your choice over the bagels.
7. Place the bagels in the air fryer basket and cook for 10 minutes or until they are golden brown and crispy.
8. Once the bagels are done, remove them from the air fryer and let them cool for a few minutes before slicing and serving.

Air Fryer Cinnamon Sugar Churros

Prep time: 10 minutes

Cook Time: 10 minutes

Serves: 4

Ingredients
- 1 cup (240 ml) water
- ½ cup (120 ml) unsalted butter
- 2 tbsp (25 g) granulated sugar
- ¼ tsp (1. 25 ml) salt
- 1 cup (125 g) all-purpose flour
- 2 large eggs
- ¼ cup (50 g) granulated sugar
- 1 tsp (5 ml) ground cinnamon
- Cooking spray

Preparation Instructions
1. In a medium saucepan, combine water, unsalted butter, granulated sugar, and salt. Heat over medium heat until the butter has melted and the mixture comes to a boil.
2. Add the flour to the saucepan and stir until a dough forms. Remove the saucepan from the heat.
3. Add the eggs to the dough one at a time, stirring well after each addition. Continue stirring until the dough becomes smooth and shiny.
4. Preheat the air fryer to 200°C.
5. Coat the air fryer basket with cooking spray.
6. Fill a pastry bag with the churro dough.
7. Pipe the dough into 4-inch (10 cm) long strips in the air fryer basket, leaving enough space between them.
8. Cook for 6-8 minutes or until the churros are golden brown and crispy.
9. In a small bowl, mix the granulated sugar and ground cinnamon.
10. Once the churros are done, remove them

from the air fryer basket and toss them in the cinnamon sugar mixture until they are coated evenly.

11. Serve immediately.

French Toast

Prep time: 5 mins

Cook Time: 5- 7 mins

Serves: 2

Ingredients

- 2 eggs
- 120 ml milk
- 1 tsp vanilla extract
- 1/2 tsp cinnamon
- 4 slices bread
- Butter, for spreading

Preparation Instructions

1. Preheat your air fryer to 180C.
2. In a small bowl, whisk together the eggs, milk, vanilla extract, and cinnamon.
3. Dip each slice of bread into the egg mixture, making sure to coat both sides evenly.
4. Spread a thin layer of butter on one side of each slice of bread.
5. Place the bread in the air fryer basket, butter side down, and cook for 5-7 minutes, or until the French toast is golden brown.

Breakfast Quinoa

Prep time: 15 mins

Cook Time: 25 mins

Serves: 2

Ingredients

- 185 g quinoa
- 240 ml water
- 30 g diced veggies (such as peppers, onions, and mushrooms)
- 45 g diced ham
- 25 g shredded cheese.

Preparation Instructions

1. Preheat your air fryer to 180C.
2. In a small saucepan, bring the water to a boil.
3. Add the quinoa and stir.
4. Reduce the heat to low and simmer for 15 minutes, or until the quinoa is cooked.
5. Stir in the veggies, ham, and cheese.
6. Transfer the mixture to a cake tin and put the tin into the air fryer basket and cook for 5-7 minutes, or until heated through and the cheese is melted.

Banana & Peanut butter Bagel

Prep time: 2 minutes

Cook Time: 6 minutes

Serves 2

Ingredients

- 2 cinnamon and raisin bagels
- 4 tsp olive margarine
- 2 tbsp crunchy peanut butter
- 2 large bananas

Preparation Instructions

1. Using a kitchen knife, cut the bagels horizontally to create 2 sliced halves
2. Spread 1 tsp of margarine on the inside of each sliced bagels
3. Place the bagels in the air fryer at 200°C for 6-7 minutes (crust layers facing down)
4. Meanwhile, peel and mash the bananas and set aside as 2 portions
5. Remove the bagels from the air fryer and put them on a plate (1 bagel per plate)
6. Inside each bagel, layer one side with 1 tbsp of peanut butter and the other side with mashed banana
7. Sandwich the bagel together and serve

Breakfast Energy Balls

Prep time: 5 mins

Cook Time: 5 - 7 mins

Serves: 5

Ingredients

- 80 g rolled oats
- 70 g almond butter
- 130 g honey
- 1 tsp vanilla extract
- 35 g chocolate chips
- 25 g shredded coconut

Preparation Instructions

1. In a medium bowl, mix together the oats, almond butter, honey, vanilla extract, chocolate chips, and coconut.
2. Roll the mixture into balls and place them in the air fryer basket.
3. Preheat your air fryer to 180C and cook the balls for 5-7 minutes, or until heated through.

Spinach Omelet

Prep time: 5 minutes

Cook Time: 12 minutes

Serves 2

Ingredients

- 4 large eggs
- 30 g chopped fresh spinach leaves
- 2 tablespoons peeled and chopped yellow onion
- 2 tablespoons salted butter, melted
- 60 g shredded mild Cheddar cheese
- ¼ teaspoon salt

Preparation Instructions

1. In an ungreased round nonstick baking dish, whisk eggs. Stir in spinach, onion, butter, Cheddar, and salt.

2. Place dish into air fryer basket. Adjust the temperature to 160ºC and bake for 12 minutes. Omelet will be done when browned on the top and firm in the middle.
3. Slice in half and serve warm on two medium plates.

Veggie Frittata

Prep time: 7 minutes

Cook Time: 21 to 23 minutes

Serves 2

Ingredients

- Avocado oil spray
- 30 g diced red onion
- 30 g diced red bell pepper
- 30 g finely chopped broccoli
- 4 large eggs
- 85 g shredded sharp Cheddar cheese, divided
- ½ teaspoon dried thyme
- Sea salt and freshly ground black pepper, to taste

Preparation Instructions

1. Spray a pan well with oil. Put the onion, pepper, and broccoli in the pan, place the pan in the air fryer, and set to 176ºC. Bake for 5 minutes.
2. While the vegetables cook, beat the eggs in a medium bowl. Stir in half of the cheese, and season with the thyme, salt, and pepper.
3. Add the eggs to the pan and top with the remaining cheese. Set the air fryer to 176ºC. Bake for 16 to 18 minutes, until cooked through.

Breakfast Pita

Prep time: 5 minutes

Cook Time: 6 minutes

Serves 2

Ingredients

- 1 whole wheat pita
- 2 teaspoons olive oil
- ½ shallot, diced
- ¼ teaspoon garlic, minced
- 1 large egg
- ¼ teaspoon dried oregano
- ¼ teaspoon dried thyme
- ⅛ teaspoon salt
- 2 tablespoons shredded Parmesan cheese

Preparation Instructions

1. Preheat the air fryer to 192ºC.
2. Brush the top of the pita with olive oil, then spread the diced shallot and minced garlic over the pita.
3. Crack the egg into a small bowl or ramekin, and season it with oregano, thyme, and salt.
4. Place the pita into the air fryer basket, and gently pour the egg onto the top of the pita. Sprinkle with cheese over the top.
5. Bake for 6 minutes.
6. Allow to cool for 5 minutes before cutting into pieces for serving.

Cheddar Eggs

Prep time: 5 minutes

Cook Time: 15 minutes

Serves 2

Ingredients

- 4 large eggs
- 2 tablespoons unsalted butter, melted
- 120 ml shredded sharp Cheddar cheese

Preparation Instructions

1. Crack eggs into a round baking dish and whisk. Place dish into the air fryer basket.
2. Adjust the temperature to 204ºC and set the timer for 10 minutes.
3. After 5 minutes, stir the eggs and add the butter and cheese. Let cook 3 more minutes and stir again.
4. Allow eggs to finish cooking an additional 2 minutes or remove if they are to your desired liking. 5. Use a fork to fluff. Serve warm.

Egg in a Hole

Prep time: 5 minutes

Cook Time: 5 minutes

Serves 1

Ingredients

- 1 slice bread
- 1 teaspoon butter, softened
- 1 egg
- Salt and pepper, to taste
- 1 tablespoon shredded Cheddar cheese
- 2 teaspoons diced ham

Preparation Instructions

1. Preheat the air fryer to 166ºC. Place a baking dish in the air fryer basket.
2. On a flat work surface, cut a hole in the center of the bread slice with a 2½-inch-diameter biscuit cutter.
3. Spread the butter evenly on each side of the bread slice and transfer to the baking dish.
4. Crack the egg into the hole and season as desired with salt and pepper. Scatter the shredded cheese and diced ham on top.
5. Bake in the preheated air fryer for 5 minutes until the bread is lightly browned and the egg is cooked to your preference.
6. Remove from the basket and serve hot.

Oat and Chia Porridge

Prep time: 10 minutes / Cook Time: 5 minutes / Serves 4

Ingredients

- 2 tablespoons peanut butter
- 4 tablespoons honey
- 1 tablespoon butter, melted
- 1 L milk
- 475 ml oats
- 235 ml chia seeds

Preparation Instructions

1. Preheat the air fryer to 200°C.
2. Put the peanut butter, honey, butter, and milk in a bowl and stir to mix. Add the oats and chia seeds and stir.
3. Transfer the mixture to a bowl and bake in the air fryer for 5 minutes. Give another stir before serving.

Simple and Easy Croutons

Prep time: 5 minutes

Cook Time: 8 minutes

Serves 4

Ingredients

- 2 slices bread
- 1 tablespoon olive oil
- Hot soup, for serving

Preparation Instructions

1. Preheat the air fryer to 200°C.
2. Cut the slices of bread into medium-size chunks.
3. Brush the air fryer basket with the oil.
4. Place the chunks inside and air fry for at least 8 minutes.
5. Serve with hot soup.

Cheesy Chilli Toast

Prep time: 5 minutes

Cook Time: 5 minutes

Serves 1

Ingredients

- 2 tablespoons grated Parmesan cheese

- 2 tablespoons grated Mozzarella cheese
- 2 teaspoons salted butter, at room temperature
- 10 to 15 thin slices serrano chilli or jalapeño
- 2 slices sourdough bread
- ½ teaspoon black pepper

Preparation Instructions

1. Preheat the air fryer to 164°C.
2. In a small bowl, stir together the Parmesan, Mozzarella, butter, and chillies.
3. Spread half the mixture onto one side of each slice of bread. Sprinkle with the pepper.
4. Place the slices, cheese-side up, in the air fryer basket. Bake for 5 minutes, or until the cheese has melted and started to brown slightly.
5. Serve immediately.

Baked Cheese Sandwich

Prep time: 5 minutes

Cook Time: 8 minutes

Serves 2

Ingredients

- 2 tablespoons mayonnaise
- 4 thick slices sourdough bread
- 4 thick slices Brie cheese
- 8 slices hot capicola or prosciutto

Preparation Instructions

1. Preheat the air fryer to 204°C. Line the air fryer basket with parchment paper.
2. In a medium bowl, stir together the melted butter and brown sugar until blended.
3. Toss the sweet potatoes in the butter mixture until coated. Place the sweet potatoes on the parchment and spritz with oil. Air fry for 5 minutes.
4. Shake the basket, spritz the sweet potatoes with oil, and air fry for 5 minutes more until they're soft enough to cut with a fork.

5. Serve immediately.

Parmesan Sausage Egg Muffins

Prep time: 5 minutes

Cook Time: 20 minutes

Serves 4

Ingredients

- 170 g Italian-seasoned sausage, sliced
- 6 eggs
- 30 ml double cream
- Salt and ground black pepper, to taste
- 85 g Parmesan cheese, grated

Preparation Instructions

1. Preheat the air fryer to 176°C. Grease a muffin pan.
2. Put the sliced sausage in the muffin pan.
3. Beat the eggs with the cream in a bowl and season with salt and pepper.
4. Pour half of the mixture over the sausages in the pan.
5. Sprinkle with cheese and the remaining egg mixture.
6. Bake in the preheated air fryer for 20 minutes or until set. 7. Serve immediately.

Classic British Breakfast

Prep time: 5 minutes

Cook Time: 25 minutes

Serves 2

Ingredients

- 235 ml potatoes, sliced and diced
- 475 ml baked beans
- 2 eggs
- 1 tablespoon olive oil
- 1 sausage
- Salt, to taste

Preparation Instructions

1. Preheat the air fryer to 200°C and allow to warm.
2. Break the eggs onto a baking dish and sprinkle with salt.
3. Lay the beans on the dish, next to the eggs.
4. In a bowl, coat the potatoes with the olive oil. Sprinkle with salt.
5. Transfer the bowl of potato slices to the air fryer and bake for 10 minutes.
6. Swap out the bowl of potatoes for the dish containing the eggs and beans. Bake for another 10 minutes. Cover the potatoes with parchment paper.
7. Slice up the sausage and throw the slices on top of the beans and eggs. Bake for another 5 minutes.
8. Serve with the potatoes.

Onion Omelette

Prep time: 10 minutes

Cook Time: 12 minutes

Serves 2

Ingredients

- 3 eggs
- Salt and ground black pepper, to taste
- ½ teaspoons soy sauce
- 1 large onion, chopped
- 2 tablespoons grated Cheddar cheese
- Cooking spray

Preparation Instructions

1. Preheat the air fryer to 180°C.
2. In a bowl, whisk together the eggs, salt, pepper, and soy sauce.
3. Spritz a small pan with cooking spray. Spread the chopped onion across the bottom of the pan, then transfer the pan to the air fryer.
4. Bake in the preheated air fryer for 6 minutes

or until the onion is translucent.

5. Add the egg mixture on top of the onions to coat well. Add the cheese on top, then continue baking for another 6 minutes.
6. Allow to cool before serving.

Air Fryer Breakfast Burrito

Servings: 1

Cooking Time: 10 minutes

Ingredients

- 1 whole wheat tortilla
- 2 egg whites
- 45 g black beans , rinsed and drained
- 35 g chopped tomato
- 40 g chopped onion
- 30 g shredded cheddar cheese
- Salt and pepper to taste

Preparation Instructions

1. Preheat the air fryer to 180°C.
2. In a bowl, whisk the egg whites, salt, and pepper until well combined.
3. Heat a non-stick pan over medium heat, spray with cooking spray, and pour in the egg mixture. Cook until set, then cut into small pieces.
4. Place the tortilla in the air fryer basket and add the cooked egg whites, black beans, tomato, onion, and cheese.
5. Roll up the tortilla and place it in the air fryer basket. Cook for 5 minutes or until the tortilla is crispy.

Nutrition per serving:

Calories: 340

Fat: 12g

Sodium: 540mg

Carbohydrates: 38g

Fibre: 10g

Sugars: 3g

Protein: 25g

Air Fryer Cinnamon French Toast

Servings: 1

Cooking Time: 10 minutes

Ingredients

- 2 slices of whole wheat bread
- 1 egg
- 60 ml unsweetened almond milk
- 1/2 tsp ground cinnamon
- 1/4 tsp vanilla extract
- Cooking spray
- Sugar-free maple syrup, for serving (optional)

Preparation Instructions

1. Preheat the air fryer to 180°C.
2. In a bowl, whisk the egg, almond milk, ground cinnamon, and vanilla extract until well combined.
3. Dip each slice of bread into the egg mixture until fully coated.
4. Spray the air fryer basket with cooking spray and place the bread slices in the basket.
5. Cook for 5 minutes, then flip the bread slices and cook for an additional 5 minutes.
6. Serve with Sugar-free maple syrup, if desired.

Nutrition per serving:

Calories: 231kcal

Carbohydrates: 25g

Sugars: 13g

Protein: 15g

Fat: 8g

Sodium: 351mg

Fibre: 5g

Air Fryer Breakfast Sausage Patties

Servings: 4

Cooking Time: 10 minutes

Ingredients

- 250g turkey mince
- 1 tsp dried sage
- 1/2 tsp garlic powder
- 1/2 tsp onion powder
- Salt and pepper to taste
- Cooking spray

Preparation Instructions

1. Preheat the air fryer to 200°C.
2. In a mixing bowl, combine the turkey mince, sage, garlic powder, onion powder, salt, and pepper.
3. Form the sausage mixture into 8 equal-sized patties.
4. Spray the air fryer basket with cooking spray and place the sausage patties in a single layer.
5. Cook for 5-7 minutes or until the sausage patties are browned and cooked through.
6. Remove from the air fryer and let cool for a few minutes before serving.

Nutrition per serving (2 patties):

Calories: 149kcal

Carbohydrates: 1g

Sugars: 0. 1 g

Protein: 18g

Fat: 8g Sodium: 404mg

Fibre: 0g

Homemade Cherry Breakfast Tarts

Prep time: 15 minutes

Cook Time: 20 minutes

Serves 6

Ingredients

Tarts:

- 2 refrigerated piecrusts
- 80 ml cherry preserves
- 1 teaspoon cornflour
- Cooking oil

Frosting:

- 120 ml vanilla yoghurt
- 30 g cream cheese
- 1 teaspoon stevia
- Rainbow sprinkles

Preparation Instructions

Make the Tarts

1. Place the piecrusts on a flat surface. Using a knife or pizza cutter, cut each piecrust into 3 rectangles, for 6 total. (I discard the unused dough left from slicing the edges.)
2. In a small bowl, combine the preserves and cornflour. Mix well.
3. Scoop 1 tablespoon of the preserves mixture onto the top half of each piece of piecrust.
4. Fold the bottom of each piece up to close the tart. Using the back of a fork, press along the edges of each tart to seal.
5. Spray the breakfast tarts with cooking oil and place them in the air fryer. I do not recommend stacking the breakfast tarts. They will stick together if stacked. You may need to prepare them in two batches. Bake at 375°F for 10 minutes.
6. Allow the breakfast tarts to cool fully before removing from the air fryer.
7. If necessary, repeat steps 5 and 6 for the remaining breakfast tarts.

Make the Frosting

8. In a small bowl, combine the yoghurt, cream cheese, and stevia. Mix well.
9. Spread the breakfast tarts with frosting and top with sprinkles, and serve.

Chapter 2 Poultry

Air Fryer Crispy Chicken Thighs

Prep time: 5 minutes

Cooking Time: 18-20 minutes

Serves: 4 people

Ingredients:
- 4 chicken thighs, bone-in and skin-on (approx. 450 g)
- 140g flour
- 10g paprika
- 5g garlic powder
- 5g dried thyme
- Salt and pepper, to taste
- 2 eggs, beaten
- 140g Panko breadcrumbs

Preparation Instructions
1. Preheat the air fryer to 200°C.
2. In a large bowl, mix together the flour, paprika, garlic powder, thyme, salt, and pepper.
3. In a separate bowl, beat the eggs.
4. Place the Panko breadcrumbs in another shallow dish.
5. Coat each chicken thigh in the flour mixture, then dip into the beaten eggs and finally into the Panko breadcrumbs.
6. Place the coated chicken thighs in the air fryer basket, leaving a little space between each piece.
7. Cook for 18-20 minutes, flipping the chicken halfway through cooking, until crispy and golden brown.
8. Serve hot with your favourite dipping sauce and sides.

Air Fryer BBQ Pulled Chicken

Prep time: 10 minutes

Cooking Time: 20-25 minutes

Serves: 4 people

Ingredients:
- 4 boneless, skinless chicken breasts (approx. 700 g)
- 25ml BBQ sauce
- 60ml ketchup
- 1 tbsp honey
- 2 tsp apple cider vinegar
- 1 tsp smoked paprika
- 1 tsp garlic powder
- Salt and pepper, to taste

Preparation Instructions
1. In a mixing bowl, whisk together BBQ sauce, ketchup, honey, apple cider vinegar, smoked paprika, garlic powder, salt, and pepper.
2. Add chicken breasts to the bowl and coat evenly with the sauce mixture.
3. Place the chicken in the air fryer basket and cook at 190°C for 20-25 minutes, flipping the chicken halfway through cooking.
4. Once cooked, remove the chicken from the air fryer and allow it to cool for 5 minutes.
5. Using two forks, shred the chicken into bite-sized pieces.
6. Serve the pulled chicken on a bun with additional BBQ sauce, coleslaw, or your favourite toppings. Enjoy!

Air Fryer Lemon Pepper Chicken Breasts

Prep time: 10 minutes

Cooking Time: 15-18 minutes

Serves: 4 people

Ingredients:
- 4 boneless, skinless chicken breasts (about 450 g)
- 1/2 tsp freshly ground black pepper
- 1 tsp salt
- 1 tsp dried thyme
- 2 tbsp olive oil
- 2 tbsp lemon juice
- 1 tbsp lemon zest
- 1 tsp garlic powder
- 1 cup Panko breadcrumbs

Preparation Instructions
1. Preheat air fryer to 200°C.
2. In a small bowl, mix together lemon zest, garlic powder, olive oil, lemon juice, salt, thyme, and black pepper.
3. Place the chicken breasts in a large bowl and cover with the lemon pepper marinade, ensuring each breast is coated well. Let the chicken marinate for 10 minutes.
4. In a shallow dish, mix together Panko breadcrumbs and remaining pepper.
5. Dip each marinated chicken breast into the breadcrumb mixture, making sure it's evenly coated.
6. Place the chicken breasts in the air fryer basket, not touching each other.
7. Cook for 15-18 minutes or until the internal temperature reaches 73. 9°C.
8. Serve the lemon pepper chicken with your favourite sides. Enjoy!

Air Fryer Buffalo Chicken Wontons

Prep time: 20 minutes

Cook Time: 8-10 minutes

Serves: 4

Ingredients:
- 1 cup (150g) cooked chicken, shredded
- ¼ cup (60g) cream cheese, softened
- ¼ cup (60g) buffalo sauce
- ¼ cup (30g) crumbled blue cheese
- 2 green onions, thinly sliced
- ¼ tsp garlic powder
- Salt and pepper, to taste
- 16 wonton wrappers
- Cooking spray

Preparation Instructions
1. Preheat the air fryer to 190°C.
2. In a mixing bowl, combine the shredded chicken, cream cheese, buffalo sauce, blue cheese, green onions, garlic powder, salt and pepper.
3. Place a tablespoon of the chicken mixture in the center of each wonton wrapper.
4. Brush the edges of the wonton wrapper with water and fold it in half to form a triangle shape, pressing the edges together to seal.
5. Repeat the process until all the wonton wrappers are filled.
6. Lightly spray the wontons with cooking spray.
7. Place the wontons in the air fryer basket in a single layer.
8. Cook for 8-10 minutes or until golden brown, flipping them over halfway through the Cooking Time.
9. Once done, remove the wontons from the air fryer and serve them hot with extra buffalo sauce and blue cheese for dipping.

Chicken Schnitzel Dogs

Prep time: 15 minutes

Cook Time: 8 to 10 minutes

Serves 4

Ingredients:

- 60 g plain flour
- ½ teaspoon salt
- 1 teaspoon marjoram
- 1 teaspoon dried parsley flakes
- ½ teaspoon thyme
- 1 egg
- 1 teaspoon lemon juice
- 1 teaspoon water
- 125 g bread crumbs
- 4 chicken breast fillets, pounded thin
- Oil for misting or cooking spray
- 4 whole grain hotdog buns
- 4 slices Gouda cheese
- 1 small Granny Smith apple, thinly sliced
- 60 g shredded Savoy cabbage
- Coleslaw dressing

Preparation Instructions

1. In a shallow dish, mix together the flour, salt, marjoram, parsley, and thyme.
2. In another shallow dish, beat together egg, lemon juice, and water.
3. Place bread crumbs in a third shallow dish.
4. Cut each of the flattened chicken fillets in half lengthwise.
5. Dip flattened chicken strips in flour mixture, then egg wash. Let excess egg drip off and roll in bread crumbs. Spray both sides with oil or cooking spray.
6. Air fry at 200ºC for 5 minutes. Spray with oil, turn over, and spray other side.
7. Cook for 3 to 5 minutes more, until well done and crispy brown.
8. To serve, place 2 schnitzel strips on bottom of each hotdog bun. Top with cheese, sliced

apple, and cabbage. Drizzle with coleslaw dressing and top with other half of bun.

Kung Pao Chicken

Prep time: 5 mins

Cook Time: 8 -10 mins

Serves: 4

Ingredients:

- 500g boneless, skinless chicken thighs, diced
- 2 tablespoons cornflour
- 2 tablespoons soy sauce
- 1 tablespoon rice vinegar
- 2 teaspoons sugar
- 1 teaspoon sesame oil
- 2 cloves of garlic, minced
- 1 teaspoon grated ginger
- 1/4 teaspoon red pepper flakes
- 2 tablespoons vegetable oil
- 1 red pepper, diced
- 30 g unsalted peanuts

Ingredients:

1. In a mixing bowl, combine the chicken, cornflour, soy sauce, rice vinegar, sugar, sesame oil, garlic, ginger, and red pepper flakes. Mix well.
2. Preheat your air fryer to 180C.
3. Place the chicken in a single layer in the air fryer and cook for 8-10 minutes or until cooked through.

Italian Flavour Chicken Breasts

Prep time: 10 minutes

Cook Time: 60 minutes

Serves 8

Ingredients:

- 1. 4 kg chicken breasts, bone-in

- 1 teaspoon minced fresh basil
- 1 teaspoon minced fresh rosemary
- 2 tablespoons minced fresh parsley
- 1 teaspoon cayenne pepper
- ½ teaspoon salt
- ½ teaspoon freshly ground black pepper
- 4 medium Roma tomatoes, halved
- Cooking spray

Preparation Instructions

1. Preheat the air fryer to 190ºC. Spritz the air fryer basket with cooking spray.
2. Combine all the Ingredients, except for the chicken breasts and tomatoes, in a large bowl. Stir to mix well.
3. Dunk the chicken breasts in the mixture and press to coat well.
4. Transfer the chicken breasts in the preheated air fryer. You may need to work in batches to avoid overcrowding.
5. Air fry for 25 minutes or until the internal temperature of the thickest part of the breasts reaches at least 76ºC. Flip the breasts halfway through the Cooking Time.
6. Remove the cooked chicken breasts from the basket and adjust the temperature to 180ºC.
7. Place the tomatoes in the air fryer and spritz with cooking spray. Sprinkle with a touch of salt and cook for 10 minutes or until tender. Shake the basket halfway through the Cooking Time.
8. Serve the tomatoes with chicken breasts on a large serving plate.

Chicken Breasts with Asparagus, Beans, and Rocket

Prep time: 20 minutes

Cook Time: 25 minutes

Serves 2

Ingredients:

- 125 g canned cannellini beans, rinsed
- 1½ tablespoons red wine vinegar
- 1 garlic clove, minced
- 2 tablespoons extra-virgin olive oil, divided
- Salt and ground black pepper, to taste
- ½ red onion, sliced thinly
- 230 g asparagus, trimmed and cut into 1-inch lengths
- 2 (230 g) boneless, skinless chicken breasts, trimmed
- ¼ teaspoon paprika
- ½ teaspoon ground coriander
- 60 g baby rocket, rinsed and drained

Preparation Instructions

1. Preheat the air fryer to 204ºC.
2. Warm the beans in microwave for 1 minutes and combine with red wine vinegar, garlic, 1 tablespoon of olive oil, ¼ teaspoon of salt, and ¼ teaspoon of ground black pepper in a bowl. Stir to mix well.
3. Combine the onion with ⅛ teaspoon of salt, ⅛ teaspoon of ground black pepper, and 2 teaspoons of olive oil in a separate bowl. Toss to coat well.
4. Place the onion in the air fryer and air fry for 2 minutes, then add the asparagus and air fry for 8 more minutes or until the asparagus is tender. Shake the basket halfway through. Transfer the onion and asparagus to the bowl with beans. Set aside.
5. Toss the chicken breasts with remaining Ingredients, except for the baby arugula, in a large bowl.
6. Put the chicken breasts in the air fryer and air fry for 14 minutes or until the internal temperature of the chicken reaches at least 76ºC. Flip the breasts halfway through.
7. Remove the chicken from the air fryer and serve on an aluminum foil with asparagus, beans, onion, and rocket. Sprinkle with salt and ground black pepper. Toss to serve.

Crisp Paprika Chicken Drumsticks

Prep time: 5 minutes

Cook Time: 22 minutes

Serves 2

Ingredients:

- 2 teaspoons paprika
- 1 teaspoon packed brown sugar
- 1 teaspoon garlic powder
- ½ teaspoon dry mustard
- ½ teaspoon salt
- Pinch pepper
- 4 (140 g) chicken drumsticks, trimmed
- 1 teaspoon vegetable oil
- 1 spring onion, green part only, sliced thin on bias

Preparation Instructions

1. Preheat the air fryer to 204°C.
2. Combine paprika, sugar, garlic powder, mustard, salt, and pepper in a bowl. Pat drumsticks dry with paper towels. Using metal skewer, poke 10 to 15 holes in skin of each drumstick. Rub with oil and sprinkle evenly with spice mixture.
3. Arrange drumsticks in air fryer basket, spaced evenly apart, alternating ends. Air fry until chicken is crisp and registers 92°C, 22 to 25 minutes, flipping chicken halfway through cooking.
4. Transfer chicken to serving platter, tent loosely with aluminum foil, and let rest for 5 minutes. Sprinkle with spring onion and serve.

Thai-Style Cornish Game Hens

Prep time: 30 minutes

Cook Time: 20 minutes

Serves 4

Ingredients:

- 20 g chopped fresh coriander leaves and stems
- 60 g fish sauce
- 1 tablespoon soy sauce
- 1 Serrano chilli, seeded and chopped
- 8 garlic cloves, smashed
- 2 tablespoons sugar
- 2 tablespoons lemongrass paste
- 2 teaspoons black pepper
- 2 teaspoons ground coriander
- 1 teaspoon kosher or coarse sea salt
- 1 teaspoon ground turmeric
- 2 Cornish game hens, giblets removed, split in half lengthwise

Preparation Instructions

1. In a blender, combine the coriander, fish sauce, soy sauce, Serrano, garlic, sugar, lemongrass, black pepper, coriander, salt, and turmeric. Blend until smooth.
2. Place the game hen halves in a large bowl. Pour the cilantro mixture over the hen halves and toss to coat. Marinate at room temperature for 30 minutes, or cover and refrigerate for up to 24 hours.
3. Arrange the hen halves in a single layer in the air fryer basket. Set the air fryer to 204°C for 20 minutes. Use a meat thermometer to ensure the game hens have reached an internal temperature of 76°C.

Whole Chicken Roast

Prep time: 10 minutes

Cook Time: 1 hour

Serves 6

Ingredients:

- 1 teaspoon salt
- 1 teaspoon Italian seasoning
- ½ teaspoon freshly ground black pepper

- ½ teaspoon paprika
- ½ teaspoon garlic powder
- ½ teaspoon onion powder
- 2 tablespoons olive oil, plus more as needed

1 (1. 8 kg) small chicken

Preparation Instructions

1. Preheat the air fryer to 182ºC.
2. Grease the air fryer basket lightly with olive oil. In a small bowl, mix the salt, Italian seasoning, pepper, paprika, garlic powder, and onion powder.
3. Remove any giblets from the chicken. Pat the chicken dry thoroughly with paper towels, including the cavity.
4. Brush the chicken all over with the olive oil and rub it with the seasoning mixture.
5. Truss the chicken or tie the legs with butcher's twine. This will make it easier to flip the chicken during cooking.
6. Put the chicken in the air fryer basket, breast-side down. Air fry for 30 minutes.
7. Flip the chicken over and baste it with any drippings collected in the bottom drawer of the air fryer.
8. Lightly brush the chicken with olive oil. Air fry for 20 minutes.
9. Flip the chicken over one last time and air fry until a thermometer inserted into the thickest part of the thigh reaches at least 74ºC and it's crispy and golden, 10 more minutes. Continue to cook, checking every 5 minutes until the chicken reaches the correct internal temperature.
10. Let the chicken rest for 10 minutes before carving and serving.

Old Bay Chicken Wings

Prep time: 10 minutes

Cook Time: 12 to 15 minutes

Serves 4

Ingredients:

- 2 tablespoons Old Bay or all-purpose seasoning
- 2 teaspoons baking powder
- 2 teaspoons salt
- 900 g chicken wings, patted dry
- Cooking spray

Preparation Instructions

1. Preheat the air fryer to 204ºC. Lightly spray the air fryer basket with cooking spray.
2. Combine the seasoning, baking powder, and salt in a large zip-top plastic bag. Add the chicken wings, seal, and shake until the wings are thoroughly coated in the seasoning mixture.
3. Lay the chicken wings in the air fryer basket in a single layer and lightly mist with cooking spray. You may need to work in batches to avoid overcrowding.
4. Air fry for 12 to 15 minutes, flipping the wings halfway through, or until the wings are lightly browned and the internal temperature reaches at least 74ºC on a meat thermometer.
5. Remove from the basket to a plate and repeat with the remaining chicken wings.
6. Serve hot.

Chicken Rumaki

Prep time: 30 minutes

Cook Time: 10 to 12 minutes per batch

Makes about 24 rumaki

Ingredients:

- 283 g raw chicken livers
- 1 can sliced water chestnuts, drained
- 60 ml low-salt teriyaki sauce
- 12 slices turkey bacon

Preparation Instructions

1. Cut livers into 1½-inch pieces, trimming out

tough veins as you slice.

2. Place livers, water chestnuts, and teriyaki sauce in small container with lid. If needed, add another tablespoon of teriyaki sauce to make sure livers are covered. Refrigerate for 1 hour.

3. When ready to cook, cut bacon slices in half crosswise.

4. Wrap 1 piece of liver and 1 slice of water chestnut in each bacon strip. Secure with toothpick.

5. When you have wrapped half of the livers, place them in the air fryer basket in a single layer.

6. Air fry at 200°C for 10 to 12 minutes, until liver is done, and bacon is crispy.

7. While first batch cooks, wrap the remaining livers. Repeat step 6 to cook your second batch.

Cajun-Breaded Chicken Bites

Prep time: 10 minutes

Cook Time: 12 minutes

Serves 4

Ingredients:

- 450 g boneless, skinless chicken breasts, cut into 1-inch cubes
- 120 g heavy whipping cream
- ½ teaspoon salt
- ¼ teaspoon ground black pepper
- 30 g plain pork rinds, finely crushed
- 40 g unflavoured whey protein powder
- ½ teaspoon Cajun seasoning

Preparation Instructions

1. Place chicken in a medium bowl and pour in cream. Stir to coat. Sprinkle with salt and pepper.

2. In a separate large bowl, combine pork rinds, protein powder, and Cajun seasoning. Remove chicken from cream, shaking off any excess, and toss in dry mix until fully coated.

3. Place bites into ungreased air fryer basket. Adjust the temperature to 200°C and air fry for 12 minutes, shaking the basket twice during cooking. Bites will be done when golden brown and have an internal temperature of at least 76°C. Serve warm.

French Garlic Chicken

Prep time: 30 minutes

Cook Time: 27 minutes

Serves 4

Ingredients:

- 2 tablespoon extra-virgin olive oil
- 1 tablespoon Dijon mustard
- 1 tablespoon apple cider vinegar
- 3 cloves garlic, minced
- 2 teaspoons herbes de Provence
- ½ teaspoon kosher salt
- 1 teaspoon black pepper
- 450 g boneless, skinless chicken thighs, halved crosswise
- 2 tablespoons butter
- 8 cloves garlic, chopped
- 60 g heavy whipping cream

Preparation Instructions

1. In a small bowl, combine the olive oil, mustard, vinegar, minced garlic, herbes de Provence, salt, and pepper. Use a wire whisk to emulsify the mixture.

2. Pierce the chicken all over with a fork to allow the marinade to penetrate better. Place the chicken in a resealable plastic bag, pour the marinade over, and seal. Massage until the chicken is well coated. Marinate at room temperature for 30 minutes or in the refrigerator for up to 24 hours.

3. When you are ready to cook, place the butter and chopped garlic in a baking pan and place it in the air fryer basket. Set the air fryer to

200ºC for 5 minutes, or until the butter has melted and the garlic is sizzling.

4. Add the chicken and the marinade to the seasoned butter. Set the air fryer to 180ºC for 15 minutes. Use a meat thermometer to ensure the chicken has reached an internal temperature of 76ºC. Transfer the chicken to a plate and cover lightly with foil to keep warm.

5. Add the cream to the pan, stirring to combine with the garlic, butter, and cooking juices. Place the pan in the air fryer basket. Set the air fryer to 180ºC for 7 minutes.

6. Pour the thickened sauce over the chicken and serve.

Chicken Chimichangas

Prep time: 20 minutes

Cook Time: 8 to 10 minutes

Serves 4

Ingredients:

- 280 g cooked chicken, shredded
- 2 tablespoons chopped green chilies
- ½ teaspoon oregano
- ½ teaspoon cumin
- ½ teaspoon onion powder
- ¼ teaspoon garlic powder
- Salt and pepper, to taste
- 8 flour tortillas (6- or 7-inch diameter)
- Oil for misting or cooking spray
- Chimichanga Sauce:
- 2 tablespoons butter
- 2 tablespoons flour
- 235 ml chicken broth
- 60 g light sour cream
- ¼ teaspoon salt
- 60 g Pepper Jack or Monterey Jack cheese, shredded

Preparation Instructions

1. Make the sauce by melting butter in a saucepan over medium-low heat. Stir in flour until smooth and slightly bubbly. Gradually add broth, stirring constantly until smooth. Cook and stir 1 minute, until the mixture slightly thickens. Remove from heat and stir in sour cream and salt. Set aside.

2. In a medium bowl, mix together the chicken, chilies, oregano, cumin, onion powder, garlic, salt, and pepper. Stir in 3 to 4 tablespoons of the sauce, using just enough to make the filling moist but not soupy.

3. Divide filling among the 8 tortillas. Place filling down the centre of tortilla, stopping about 1 inch from edges. Fold one side of tortilla over filling, fold the two sides in, and then roll up. Mist all sides with oil or cooking spray.

4. Place chimichangas in air fryer basket seam side down. To fit more into the basket, you can stand them on their sides with the seams against the sides of the basket.

5. Air fry at 180ºC for 8 to 10 minutes or until heated through and crispy brown outside.

6. Add the shredded cheese to the remaining sauce. Stir over low heat, warming just until the cheese melts. Don't boil or sour cream may curdle.

7. Drizzle the sauce over the chimichangas.

Air Fried Chicken Potatoes with Sun-Dried Tomato

Prep time: 15 minutes

Cook Time: 25 minutes

Serves 2

Ingredients:

- 2 teaspoons minced fresh oregano, divided
- 2 teaspoons minced fresh thyme, divided
- 2 teaspoons extra-virgin olive oil, plus extra as needed

- 450 g fingerling potatoes, unpeeled
- 2 (340 g) bone-in split chicken breasts, trimmed
- 1 garlic clove, minced
- 15 g oil-packed sun-dried tomatoes, patted dry and chopped
- 1½ tablespoons red wine vinegar
- 1 tablespoon capers, rinsed and minced
- 1 small shallot, minced
- Salt and ground black pepper, to taste

Preparation Instructions

1. Preheat the air fryer to 180ºC.
2. Combine 1 teaspoon of oregano, 1 teaspoon of thyme, ¼ teaspoon of salt, ¼ teaspoon of ground black pepper, 1 teaspoons of olive oil in a large bowl. Add the potatoes and toss to coat well.
3. Combine the chicken with remaining thyme, oregano, and olive oil. Sprinkle with garlic, salt, and pepper. Toss to coat well.
4. Place the potatoes in the preheated air fryer, then arrange the chicken on top of the potatoes.
5. Air fry for 25 minutes or until the internal temperature of the chicken reaches at least 76ºC and the potatoes are wilted. Flip the chicken and potatoes halfway through.
6. Meanwhile, combine the sun-dried tomatoes, vinegar, capers, and shallot in a separate large bowl. Sprinkle with salt and ground black pepper. Toss to mix well.
7. Remove the chicken and potatoes from the air fryer and allow to cool for 10 minutes. Serve with the sun-dried tomato mix.

Bell Pepper Stuffed Chicken Roll-Ups

Prep time: 10 minutes

Cook Time: 12 minutes

Serves 4

Ingredients:

- 2 (115 g) boneless, skinless chicken breasts, slice in half horizontally
- 1 tablespoon olive oil
- Juice of ½ lime
- 2 tablespoons taco seasoning
- ½ green bell pepper, cut into strips
- ½ red bell pepper, cut into strips
- ¼ onion, sliced

Preparation Instructions

1. Preheat the air fryer to 200ºC.
2. Unfold the chicken breast slices on a clean work surface. Rub with olive oil, then drizzle with lime juice and sprinkle with taco seasoning.
3. Top the chicken slices with equal amount of bell peppers and onion. Roll them up and secure with toothpicks.
4. Arrange the chicken roll-ups in the preheated air fryer. Air fry for 12 minutes or until the internal temperature of the chicken reaches at least 76ºC. Flip the chicken roll-ups halfway through.
5. Remove the chicken from the air fryer. Discard the toothpicks and serve immediately.

Bacon-Wrapped Chicken Breasts Rolls

Prep time: 10 minutes

Cook Time: 15 minutes

Serves 4

Ingredients:

- 15 g chopped fresh chives
- 2 tablespoons lemon juice
- 1 teaspoon dried sage
- 1 teaspoon fresh rosemary leaves
- 15 g fresh parsley leaves
- 4 cloves garlic, peeled
- 1 teaspoon ground fennel

- 3 teaspoons sea salt
- ½ teaspoon red pepper flakes
- 4 (115 g) boneless, skinless chicken breasts, pounded to ¼ inch thick
- 8 slices bacon
- Sprigs of fresh rosemary, for garnish
- Cooking spray

Preparation Instructions

1. Preheat the air fryer to 170ºC. Spritz the air fryer basket with cooking spray.
2. Put the chives, lemon juice, sage, rosemary, parsley, garlic, fennel, salt, and red pepper flakes in a food processor, then pulse to purée until smooth.
3. Unfold the chicken breasts on a clean work surface, then brush the top side of the chicken breasts with the sauce.
4. Roll the chicken breasts up from the shorter side, then wrap each chicken rolls with 2 bacon slices to cover. Secure with toothpicks.
5. Arrange the rolls in the preheated air fryer, then cook for 10 minutes. Flip the rolls halfway through.
6. Increase the heat to 200ºC and air fry for 5 more minutes or until the bacon is browned and crispy.
7. Transfer the rolls to a large plate. Discard the toothpicks and spread with rosemary sprigs before serving.

Air Fryer Chicken Parmesan

Servings: 4

Cooking Time: 20 minutes

Ingredients:

- 500g boneless, skinless chicken breasts
- 60g almond flour
- 60g grated Parmesan cheese
- 2g garlic powder

- 2g onion powder
- 2g dried basil
- 2g dried oregano
- Salt and pepper to taste
- 1 large egg, beaten
- 60g Sugar-free tomato sauce
- 60g shredded mozzarella cheese
- Fresh basil, chopped, for garnish

Preparation Instructions

1. Preheat the air fryer to 190°C.
2. Cut the chicken breasts into thin cutlets.
3. In a mixing bowl, combine the almond flour, grated Parmesan cheese, garlic powder, onion powder, dried basil, dried oregano, salt, and pepper. Mix well.
4. Dip each chicken cutlet into the beaten egg, then coat it in the almond flour mixture. Place the coated chicken onto the air fryer basket or tray.
5. Air fry the chicken for 8 minutes. Flip the chicken over, then air fry for another 5-7 minutes, or until cooked through and crispy.
6. Spoon the tomato sauce onto each chicken cutlet, then sprinkle with shredded mozzarella cheese.
7. Air fry for another 2-3 minutes, or until the cheese is melted and bubbly.
8. Garnish with fresh basil, if desired, then serve and enjoy!

Nutritional Information (per serving):

Calories: 329; Carbohydrates: 6g; Fats: 13g, Protein: 47g,Sodium: 606mg ,Fibre: 1g

Air Fryer Lemon Garlic Chicken

Cooking Time: 25 minutes

Servings: 4

Ingredients:

- 4 chicken breasts (about 600g), boneless and

- skinless
- 10g olive oil
- 3g minced garlic
- 1tsp dried oregano
- 1tsp dried basil
- 1tsp paprika
- ½ tsp salt
- ½ tsp black pepper
- 1 lemon, sliced

Preparation Instructions

1. Preheat the air fryer to 190°C.
2. Rinse the chicken breasts and pat dry with a paper towel.
3. In a small bowl, mix together the olive oil, minced garlic, oregano, basil, paprika, salt, and black pepper.
4. Brush the mixture over both sides of the chicken breasts.
5. Place the chicken breasts in the air fryer basket or tray.
6. Top each chicken breast with a slice of lemon.
7. Air fry for 20-25 minutes, or until the chicken is cooked through and the internal temperature reaches 74°C.
8. Serve the lemon garlic chicken hot with your favourite side dish.

Nutritional Information (per serving):
Calories: 202 Carbohydrates: 2g Fats: 7g Protein: 33g Sodium: 436mg Fibre: 1g

Air Fryer Chicken Fajitas

Servings: 4

Cooking Time: 20 minutes

Ingredients:

- 500g boneless, skinless chicken breasts, sliced
- 2 peppers, sliced
- 1 onion, sliced
- 2 tablespoons olive oil

- 1 tablespoon chili powder
- 1 tablespoon paprika
- 1 teaspoon garlic powder
- 1 teaspoon onion powder
- Salt and pepper to taste

Preparation Instructions

1. Preheat the air fryer to 180°C.
2. In a bowl, mix together the olive oil, chili powder, paprika, garlic powder, onion powder, salt, and pepper.
3. Add the sliced chicken, peppers, and onion to the bowl and toss until coated.
4. Place the chicken and vegetables in the air fryer basket.
5. Cook in the air fryer for 15-20 minutes, or until the chicken is cooked through and the vegetables are tender.
6. Serve hot and enjoy!

Nutritional Information (per serving):
Calories: 260 Carbs: 9g Fat: 11g Protein: 30g Sodium: 300mg Fibre: 3g

Pecan Turkey Cutlets

Prep time: 10 minutes

Cook Time: 10 to 12 minutes per batch

Serves 4

Ingredients:

- 90 g panko bread crumbs
- ¼ teaspoon salt
- ¼ teaspoon pepper
- ¼ teaspoon mustard powder
- ¼ teaspoon poultry seasoning
- 50 g pecans
- 30 g cornflour
- 1 egg, beaten
- 450 g turkey cutlets, ½-inch thick
- Salt and pepper, to taste
- Oil for misting or cooking spray

Preparation Instructions

1. Place the panko crumbs, ¼ teaspoon salt, ¼ teaspoon pepper, mustard, and poultry seasoning in food processor. Process until crumbs are finely crushed. Add pecans and process in short pulses just until nuts are finely chopped. Go easy so you don't overdo it!
2. Preheat the air fryer to 180°C.
3. Place cornflour in one shallow dish and beaten egg in another. Transfer coating mixture from food processor into a third shallow dish.
4. Sprinkle turkey cutlets with salt and pepper to taste.
5. Dip cutlets in cornflour and shake off excess. Then dip in beaten egg and roll in crumbs, pressing to coat well. Spray both sides with oil or cooking spray.
6. Place 2 cutlets in air fryer basket in a single layer and cook for 10 to 12 minutes or until juices run clear.
7. Repeat step 6 to cook remaining cutlets.

Stuffed Turkey Roulade

Prep time: 10 minutes

Cook Time: 45 minutes

Serves 4

Ingredients:

- 1 (900 g) boneless turkey breast, skin removed
- 1 teaspoon salt
- ½ teaspoon black pepper
- 115 g goat cheese
- 1 tablespoon fresh thyme
- 1 tablespoon fresh sage
- 2 garlic cloves, minced
- 2 tablespoons olive oil
- Fresh chopped parsley, for garnish

Preparation Instructions

1. Preheat the air fryer to 192°C.
2. Using a sharp knife, butterfly the turkey breast, and season both sides with salt and pepper and set aside.
3. In a small bowl, mix together the goat cheese, thyme, sage, and garlic.
4. Spread the cheese mixture over the turkey breast, then roll it up tightly, tucking the ends underneath.
5. Place the turkey breast roulade onto a piece of aluminum foil, wrap it up, and place it into the air fryer.
6. Bake for 30 minutes. Remove the foil from the turkey breast and brush the top with oil, then continue cooking for another 10 to 15 minutes, or until the outside has browned and the internal temperature reaches 76°C.
7. Remove and cut into 1-inch-wide slices and serve with a sprinkle of parsley on top.

Chicken Rochambeau

Prep time: 15 minutes

Cook Time: 20 minutes

Serves 4

Ingredients:

- 1 tablespoon butter
- 4 chicken tenders, cut in half crosswise
- Salt and pepper, to taste
- 30 g flour
- Oil for misting
- 4 slices ham, ¼- to ⅜-inches thick and large enough to cover an English muffin
- 2 English muffins, split

Sauce:
- 2 tablespoons butter
- 25 g chopped green onions
- 50 g chopped mushrooms
- 2 tablespoons flour

- 240 ml chicken broth
- ¼ teaspoon garlic powder
- 1½ teaspoons Worcestershire sauce

Preparation Instructions

1. Place 1 tablespoon of butter in a baking pan and air fry at 200°C for 2 minutes to melt.
2. Sprinkle chicken tenders with salt and pepper to taste, then roll in the flour.
3. Place chicken in baking pan, turning pieces to coat with melted butter.
4. Air fry at 200°C for 5 minutes. Turn chicken pieces over, and spray tops lightly with olive oil. Cook 5 minutes longer or until juices run clear. The chicken will not brown.
5. While chicken is cooking, make the sauce: In a medium saucepan, melt the 2 tablespoons of butter.
6. Add onions and mushrooms and sauté until tender, about 3 minutes.
7. Stir in the flour. Gradually add broth, stirring constantly until you have a smooth gravy.
8. Add garlic powder and Worcestershire sauce and simmer on low heat until sauce thickens, about 5 minutes.
9. When chicken is cooked, remove baking pan from air fryer and set aside.
10. Place ham slices directly into air fryer basket and air fry at 200°C for 5 minutes or until hot and beginning to sizzle a little. Remove and set aside on top of the chicken for now.
11. Place the English muffin halves in air fryer basket and air fry at 200°C for 1 minute.
12. Open air fryer and place a ham slice on top of each English muffin half. Stack 2 pieces of chicken on top of each ham slice. Air fry for 1 to 2 minutes to heat through.
13. Place each English muffin stack on a serving plate and top with plenty of sauce.

Tandoori chicken

Prep time: 15 minutes

Cook Time: 20 minutes

Serves: 4

Ingredients:

- 4 bone-in chicken thighs
- 400g plain Greek yoghurt
- 2 tablespoons lemon juice
- 1 tablespoon grated ginger
- 1 tablespoon garam masala
- 1 tablespoon ground cumin
- 1 tablespoon smoked paprika
- 1 tablespoon garlic powder
- Salt and pepper, to taste
- 2 teaspoons olive oil

Preparation Instructions

1. In a large bowl, whisk together the Greek yoghurt, lemon juice, grated ginger, garam masala, cumin, smoked paprika, garlic powder, salt, and pepper to form a marinade.
2. Add the chicken thighs to the marinade, making sure to coat them well. Cover and refrigerate for at least 1 hour, or overnight for best results.
3. Preheat the air fryer to 180°C.
4. Remove the chicken thighs from the marinade and shake off any excess.
5. Brush the chicken thighs with olive oil on all sides.
6. Place the chicken thighs in the air fryer basket and cook for 20 minutes, turning halfway through, or until the internal temperature reaches 75°C.
7. Let the chicken thighs rest for 5-10 minutes before serving.
8. Enjoy this delicious and flavourful tandoori chicken with your favourite sides for a delicious and satisfying meal!

Jerk chicken wings

Serves: 4

Prep time: 15 minutes

Cook Time: 20 minutes

Ingredients:

- 12 chicken wings
- 2 tbsp jerk seasoning
- 1 tbsp vegetable oil

Preparation Instructions

1. Combine the chicken wings, jerk seasoning, and vegetable oil in a mixing bowl, and toss to coat.
2. Arrange the chicken wings on the crisper plate and select "AIR FRY" at 200°C for 20 minutes.
3. Select "START STOP" to begin cooking.
4. When the timer beeps, check the chicken wings with a meat thermometer to ensure they have reached an internal temperature of 75°C.
5. Serve hot with your favourite dipping sauce.

Air fryer chicken and waffles

Prep time: 15 minutes

Cook Time: 18 minutes

Serves: 4

Ingredients:

For the chicken:

- 4 boneless, skinless chicken breasts
- 240m buttermilk
- 125g all-purpose flour
- 1 tbsp paprika
- 1 tbsp garlic powder
- 1 tbsp onion powder
- 1 tsp sea salt
- 1/2 tsp black pepper
- Cooking spray

For the waffles:

- 250g all-purpose flour
- 2 tbsp sugar
- 1 tbsp baking powder
- 1/2 tsp sea salt
- 420ml milk
- 2 eggs
- 60g unsalted butter, melted
- 1 tsp vanilla extract

Preparation Instructions

1. Preheat your air fryer to 190°C.
2. In a shallow dish, marinate the chicken breasts in buttermilk for at least 30 minutes.
3. In another shallow dish, mix the flour, paprika, garlic powder, onion powder, sea salt, and black pepper.
4. Remove the chicken breasts from the buttermilk and dredge them in the flour mixture, shaking off any excess flour.
5. Spray the air fryer basket with cooking spray and place the chicken breasts inside.
6. Spray the top of the chicken with additional cooking spray.
7. Cook for 15-20 minutes, or until the internal temperature of the chicken reaches 74°C and the coating is crispy and golden brown.
8. While the chicken is cooking, make the waffle batter.
9. In a large bowl, whisk together the flour, sugar, baking powder, and sea salt.
10. In a separate bowl, whisk together the milk, eggs, melted butter, and vanilla extract.
11. Pour the wet Ingredients into the dry Ingredients and stir until just combined.
12. Pour the waffle batter into a preheated waffle iron and cook according to the manufacturer's Instructions.
13. Serve the air fryer chicken with the waffles and your favourite toppings, such as syrup, honey, or hot sauce. Enjoy!

Chapter 3: Fish and Seafood

Air Fryer Lemon Garlic Tilapia

Prep time: 10 minutes

Cooking Time: 10-12 minutes

Serves: 4 people

Ingredients

- 4 tilapia fillets, about 175 g each
- 2 tablespoons olive oil
- 1 lemon, sliced into rounds
- 4 garlic cloves, minced
- Salt and pepper, to taste
- Fresh parsley or lemon wedges, for garnish (optional)

Preparation Instructions

1. Preheat the air fryer to 200°C.
2. Rinse the tilapia fillets and pat them dry with paper towels.
3. In a small bowl, mix together the olive oil, minced garlic, salt, and pepper.
4. Place the tilapia fillets in a single layer in the air fryer basket. Brush both sides of the fillets with the olive oil mixture.
5. Arrange the lemon rounds on top of the tilapia fillets.
6. Air fry the tilapia for 10-12 minutes, or until the internal temperature reaches 54°C and the fish is cooked through.
7. Serve hot, garnished with fresh parsley or lemon wedges if desired.
8. Enjoy this flavourful and easy Air Fryer Lemon Garlic Tilapia recipe!

Air Fryer Baja Fish Tacos

Prep time: 10 minutes

Cooking Time:12-15 minutes

Serves: 4 people

Ingredients

- 4 tilapia fillets, about 140 g each
- 120 g all-purpose flour
- 1 tsp smoked paprika
- 1 tsp garlic powder
- 1 tsp onion powder
- Salt and pepper, to taste
- 1 egg, beaten
- 120ml panko breadcrumbs
- 8 small flour tortillas
- 240ml shredded lettuce
- 1 avocado, diced
- 120ml salsa
- 120 ml sour cream
- 1 lime, cut into wedges

Preparation Instructions

1. Preheat the air fryer to 400°F (200°C).
2. In a large bowl, mix together the flour, paprika, garlic powder, onion powder, salt, and pepper.
3. In another bowl, beat the egg. In a third bowl, add the panko breadcrumbs.
4. Dip each tilapia fillet in the flour mixture, then the egg mixture, and finally the panko breadcrumbs, making sure each side is evenly coated.
5. Place the breaded tilapia fillets in the air fryer basket, making sure they are not touching.
6. Cook for 12-15 minutes, or until the tilapia is golden brown and cooked through.
7. While the tilapia is cooking, warm the tortillas in the microwave for 15-20 seconds or on a dry skillet until they are soft and pliable.
8. To assemble the tacos, place a few pieces of cooked tilapia onto each tortilla.
9. Top with shredded lettuce, diced avocado, salsa, and a dollop of sour cream.

10. Squeeze a wedge of lime over each taco, and serve immediately. Enjoy!

Air Fryer Crispy Calamari

Prep time: 10 minutes

Cooking Time: 8-10 minutes

Serves: 4 people

Ingredients

- 500 g fresh calamari, sliced into rings
- 1 cup all-purpose flour
- 2 teaspoons garlic powder
- 1 teaspoon dried oregano
- Salt and pepper, to taste
- 1 large egg
- 2 tablespoons milk
- 1 cup panko breadcrumbs
- Lemon wedges, for serving (optional)
- Aioli or tartar sauce, for serving (optional)

Preparation Instructions

1. In a shallow dish, mix together the flour, garlic powder, oregano, salt, and pepper.
2. In a separate shallow dish, whisk together the egg and milk.
3. In a third shallow dish, place the panko breadcrumbs.
4. Dip each calamari ring into the flour mixture, then into the egg mixture, and finally into the panko breadcrumbs, making sure to coat each ring well.
5. Preheat your air fryer to 400°F (200°C) for 5 minutes.
6. Place the breaded calamari rings in a single layer in the air fryer basket, making sure they don't overlap.
7. Cook the calamari for 8-10 minutes or until they are crispy and golden brown, flipping halfway through.
8. Serve the crispy calamari with lemon wedges and aioli or tartar sauce, if desired. Enjoy!

Air Fryer Crab Cakes

Prep time: 15 minutes

Cook Time: 10 minutes

Serves: 4

Ingredients

- 1 lb. (450g) crab meat, drained and picked over for shells
- ½ cup (60g) breadcrumbs
- ¼ cup (60g) mayonnaise
- 1 large egg, beaten
- 2 tbsp (30ml) Dijon mustard
- 1 tbsp (15ml) Worcestershire sauce
- ¼ cup (10g) chopped fresh parsley
- ¼ cup (10g) chopped scallions
- 1 tsp (5ml) Old Bay seasoning
- ¼ tsp (1. 25ml) salt
- ¼ tsp (1. 25ml) black pepper
- Cooking spray

Preparation Instructions

1. Preheat your air fryer to 200°C.
2. In a large mixing bowl, combine the crab meat, breadcrumbs, mayonnaise, beaten egg, Dijon mustard, Worcestershire sauce, chopped parsley, chopped scallions, Old Bay seasoning, salt, and black pepper. Mix well until all Ingredients are combined.
3. Form the crab mixture into small patties, approximately 2-3 inches (5-7. 5cm) in diameter.
4. Lightly coat the air fryer basket with cooking spray.
5. Arrange the crab cakes in the air fryer basket in a single layer, leaving a little space between each one.
6. Cook for 10 minutes or until the crab cakes are golden brown and cooked through, flipping them over halfway through the Cooking Time.
7. Once the crab cakes are done, remove them from the air fryer and serve immediately with your favorite dipping sauce.

Air Fryer Coconut Prawn with Sweet Chili Sauce

Prep time: 15 minutes

Cook Time: 8-10 minutes

Serves: 4

Ingredients

- 1 lb (454g) large prawn, peeled and deveined
- ½ cup (60g) all-purpose flour
- 2 large eggs, beaten
- 1 ½ cups (120g) panko breadcrumbs
- ½ cup (40g) shredded coconut
- Salt and pepper, to taste
- Cooking spray
- Sweet chili sauce, for serving

Preparation Instructions

1. Preheat your air fryer to 200°C.
2. Prepare three shallow bowls: one with flour, one with beaten eggs, and one with a mixture of panko breadcrumbs and shredded coconut.
3. Season the prawn with salt and pepper.
4. Dredge each prawn in the flour, shaking off any excess. Dip it in the beaten eggs, then coat it with the panko-coconut mixture, pressing it lightly to adhere.
5. Place the coated prawn in the air fryer basket in a single layer. Spray the prawn with cooking spray.
6. Cook for 8-10 minutes or until the prawn are cooked through and the coating is crispy and golden brown, flipping them over halfway through the Cooking Time.
7. Once the prawn is done, remove them from the air fryer and transfer them to a serving platter. Serve with sweet chili sauce on the side.

Air Fryer Mango Coconut Prawn Skewers

Prep time: 15 minutes

Cook Time: 10 minutes

Serves: 4

Ingredients

- 1 lb (450g) large prawn, peeled and deveined
- 1 mango, peeled and cubed
- 1 red pepper, seeded and cubed
- ¼ cup (60ml) coconut milk
- 1 tbsp (15ml) lime juice
- 1 tbsp (15ml) honey
- 1 tbsp (15ml) soy sauce
- 1 tsp (5ml) curry powder
- Salt and pepper, to taste
- 8 wooden skewers, soaked in water for at least 30 minutes

Preparation Instructions

1. Preheat your air fryer to 190°C.
2. In a large bowl, whisk together the coconut milk, lime juice, honey, soy sauce, curry powder, salt, and pepper.
3. Add the prawn, mango, and red pepper to the bowl and toss to coat evenly.
4. Thread the prawn, mango, and red pepper onto the soaked wooden skewers.
5. Place the skewers in the air fryer basket.
6. Cook for 10 minutes, or until the prawn are pink and cooked through, flipping the skewers halfway through cooking. Remove from the air fryer and let cool for a few minutes before serving.

Teriyaki Salmon

Prep time: 5 mins

Cook Time: 8 -10 mins

Serves: 4

Ingredients

- 4 (100 g) salmon fillets
- 60 g teriyaki sauce
- 2 tbsp honey
- 1 tbsp rice vinegar

- 1 tsp sesame oil
- 1 tsp grated ginger
- 1 clove garlic, minced

Preparation Instructions

1. In a small bowl, combine the teriyaki sauce, honey, rice vinegar, sesame oil, ginger, and garlic.
2. Place the salmon fillets in a shallow dish and brush the teriyaki mixture onto both sides of the fillets.
3. Place the salmon in the air fryer basket in a single layer.
4. Set the air fryer to 180°C and cook the salmon for 8-10 minutes, or until the salmon is cooked through and the skin is crispy.
5. Serve the salmon hot with your favourite side dish.

Maple Mustard Salmon

Prep time: 5 mins

Cook Time: 8 -10 mins

Serves: 4

Ingredients

- 4 (100 g) salmon fillets
- 2 tbsp dijon mustard
- 2 tbsp maple syrup
- 1 tsp dried thyme
- 1/2 tsp salt
- 1/4 tsp black pepper

Preparation Instructions

1. In a small bowl, combine the dijon mustard, maple syrup, thyme, salt, and pepper.
2. Place the salmon fillets in a shallow dish and brush the maple-mustard mixture onto both sides of the fillets.
3. Place the salmon in the air fryer basket in a single layer.
4. Set the air fryer to 180°C and cook the salmon for 8-10 minutes, or until the salmon is cooked through and the skin is crispy.
5. Serve the salmon hot with your favourite side dish.

Lemon Pepper Cod

Prep time: 5 mins

Cook Time: 8 -10 mins

Serves: 4

Ingredients

- 4 (100 g) cod fillets
- 2 tbsp olive oil
- 2 tbsp lemon juice
- 1 tsp lemon pepper seasoning
- 1/2 tsp salt
- 1/4 tsp black pepper

Preparation Instructions

1. In a small bowl, combine the olive oil, lemon juice, lemon pepper seasoning, salt, and pepper.
2. Place the cod fillets in a shallow dish and brush the lemon pepper mixture onto both sides of the fillets.
3. Place the cod in the air fryer basket in a single layer.
4. Set the air fryer to 180°C and cook the cod for 8-10 minutes, or until the cod is cooked through and flaky.

New Orleans-Style Crab Cakes

Prep time: 10 minutes

Cook Time: 8 to 10 minutes

Serves 4

Ingredients

- 160 g bread crumbs
- 2 teaspoons Creole Seasoning
- 1 teaspoon dry mustard
- 1 teaspoon salt
- 1 teaspoon freshly ground black pepper
- 185 g crab meat
- 2 large eggs, beaten
- 1 teaspoon butter, melted

- 40 g minced onion
- Cooking spray
- Pecan Tartar Sauce, for serving

Preparation Instructions

1. Preheat the air fryer to 176ºC. Line the air fryer basket with baking paper.
2. In a medium bowl, whisk the bread crumbs, Creole Seasoning, dry mustard, salt, and pepper until blended. Add the crab meat, eggs, butter, and onion. Stir until blended. Shape the crab mixture into 8 patties.
3. Place the crab cakes on the baking paper and spritz with oil.
4. Air fry for 4 minutes. Flip the cakes, spritz them with oil, and air fry for 4 to 6 minutes more until the outsides are firm and a fork inserted into the center comes out clean. Serve with the Pecan Tartar Sauce.

Apple Cider Mussels

Prep time: 10 minutes

Cook Time: 2 minutes

Serves 5

Ingredients

- 910 g mussels, cleaned and debearded
- 1 teaspoon onion powder
- 1 teaspoon ground cumin
- 1 tablespoon avocado oil
- 65 ml apple cider vinegar

Preparation Instructions

1. Mix mussels with onion powder, ground cumin, avocado oil, and apple cider vinegar.
2. Put the mussels in the air fryer and cook at 200ºC for 2 minutes.

Crab-Stuffed Avocado Boats

Prep time: 5 minutes

Cook Time: 7 minutes

Serves 4

Ingredients

- 2 medium avocados, halved and pitted
- 230 g cooked crab meat
- ¼ teaspoon Old Bay seasoning
- 2 tablespoons peeled and diced yellow onion
- 2 tablespoons mayonnaise

Preparation Instructions

1. Scoop out avocado flesh in each avocado half, leaving ½ inch around edges to form a shell. Chop scooped-out avocado.
2. In a medium bowl, combine crab meat, Old Bay seasoning, onion, mayonnaise, and chopped avocado. Place ¼ mixture into each avocado shell.
3. Place avocado boats into an ungreased air fryer basket. Adjust the temperature to 176ºC and air fry for 7 minutes. Avocado will be browned on the top and mixture will be bubbling when done. Serve warm.

Cajun Shrimp

Prep time: 15 minutes

Cook Time: 9 minutes

Serves 4

Ingredients

- Oil, for spraying
- 450 g jumbo raw shrimp, peeled and deveined
- 1 tablespoon Cajun seasoning
- 170 g cooked kielbasa, cut into thick slices
- ½ medium courgette, cut into ¼-inch-thick slices
- ½ medium yellow squash or butternut squash, cut into ¼-inch-thick slices
- 1 green pepper, seeded and cut into 1-inch pieces
- 2 tablespoons olive oil
- ½ teaspoon salt

Preparation Instructions

1. Preheat the air fryer to 204ºC.
2. Line the air fryer basket with parchment and

spray lightly with oil.

3. In a large bowl, toss together the shrimp and Cajun seasoning. Add the kielbasa, courgette, squash, pepper, olive oil, and salt and mix well.

4. Transfer the mixture to the prepared basket, taking care not to overcrowd. You may need to work in batches, depending on the size of your air fryer.

5. Cook for 9 minutes, shaking and stirring every 3 minutes.

6. Serve immediately.

Teriyaki Shrimp Skewers

Prep time: 10 minutes

Cook Time: 6 minutes

Serves 12

Ingredients

- skewered shrimp
- 1½ tablespoons mirin
- 1½ teaspoons ginger paste
- 1½ tablespoons soy sauce
- 12 large shrimp, peeled and deveined
- 1 large egg
- 180 ml panko breadcrumbs
- Cooking spray

Preparation Instructions

1. Combine the mirin, ginger paste, and soy sauce in a large bowl. Stir to mix well.

2. Dunk the shrimp in the bowl of mirin mixture, then wrap the bowl in plastic and refrigerate for 1 hour to marinate.

3. Preheat the air fryer to 204°C. Spritz the air fryer basket with cooking spray.

4. Run twelve 4-inch skewers through each shrimp.

5. Whisk the egg in the bowl of marinade to combine well. Pour the breadcrumbs on a plate.

6. Dredge the shrimp skewers in the egg mixture, then shake the excess off and roll over the breadcrumbs to coat well.

7. Arrange the shrimp skewers in the preheated air fryer and spritz with cooking spray. You need to work in batches to avoid overcrowding.

8. Air fry for 6 minutes or until the shrimp are opaque and firm. Flip the shrimp skewers halfway through. Serve immediately.

Lemon Pepper Prawns

Prep time: 15 minutes

Cook Time: 8 minutes

Serves 2

Ingredients

- Olive or vegetable oil, for spraying
- 340 g medium raw prawns, peeled and deveined
- 3 tablespoons lemon juice
- 1 tablespoon olive oil
- 1 teaspoon lemon pepper
- ¼ teaspoon paprika
- ¼ teaspoon granulated garlic

Preparation Instructions

1. Preheat the air fryer to 204°C. Line the air fryer basket with baking paper and spray lightly with oil.

2. In a medium bowl, toss together the prawns, lemon juice, olive oil, lemon pepper, paprika, and garlic until evenly coated.

3. Place the prawns in the prepared basket.

4. Cook for 6 to 8 minutes, or until pink and firm. Serve immediately.

Tuna-Stuffed Quinoa Patties

Prep time: 10 minutes

Cook Time: 15 minutes

Serves 4

Ingredients

- 35 g quinoa

- 4 slices white bread with crusts removed
- 120 ml milk
- 3 eggs
- 280 g tuna packed in olive oil, drained
- 2 to 3 lemons
- Kosher or coarse sea salt, and pepper, to taste
- 150 g panko bread crumbs
- Vegetable oil, for spraying
- Lemon wedges, for serving

Preparation Instructions

1. Rinse the quinoa in a fine-mesh sieve until the water runs clear. Bring 1 liter of salted water to a boil. Add the quinoa, cover, and reduce heat to low. Simmer the quinoa covered until most of the water is absorbed and the quinoa is tender, 15 to 20 minutes. Drain and allow to cool to room temperature. Meanwhile, soak the bread in the milk.
2. Mix the drained quinoa with the soaked bread and 2 of the eggs in a large bowl and mix thoroughly. In a medium bowl, combine the tuna, the remaining egg, and the juice and zest of 1 of the lemons. Season well with salt and pepper. Spread the panko on a plate.
3. Scoop up approximately 60 g of the quinoa mixture and flatten into a patty. Place a heaping tablespoon of the tuna mixture in the centre of the patty and close the quinoa around the tuna. Flatten the patty slightly to create an oval-shaped croquette. Dredge both sides of the croquette in the panko. Repeat with the remaining quinoa and tuna.
4. Spray the air fryer basket with oil to prevent sticking, and preheat the air fryer to 204°C. Arrange 4 or 5 of the croquettes in the basket, taking care to avoid overcrowding. Spray the tops of the croquettes with oil. Air fry for 8 minutes until the top side is browned and crispy. Carefully turn the croquettes over and spray the second side

with oil. Air fry until the second side is browned and crispy, another 7 minutes. Repeat with the remaining croquettes.
5. Serve the croquetas warm with plenty of lemon wedges for spritzing.

Southern-Style Catfish

Prep time: 10 minutes

Cook Time: 12 minutes

Serves 4

Ingredients

- 4 (200 g) catfish fillets
- 80 ml heavy whipping cream
- 1 tablespoon lemon juice
- 110 g blanched finely ground almond flour
- 2 teaspoons Old Bay seasoning
- ½ teaspoon salt
- ¼ teaspoon ground black pepper

Preparation Instructions

1. Place catfish fillets into a large bowl with cream and pour in lemon juice. Stir to coat.
2. In a separate large bowl, mix flour and Old Bay seasoning.
3. Remove each fillet and gently shake off excess cream. Sprinkle with salt and pepper. Press each fillet gently into flour mixture on both sides to coat.
4. Place fillets into ungreased air fryer basket. Adjust the temperature to 204°C and air fry for 12 minutes, turning fillets halfway through cooking. Catfish will be golden brown and have an internal temperature of at least 64°C when done. Serve warm.

Breaded Prawns Tacos

Prep time: 10 minutes

Cook Time: 9 minutes

Makes 8 tacos

Ingredients
- 2 large eggs
- 1 teaspoon prepared yellow mustard
- 455 g small prawns, peeled, deveined, and tails removed
- 45 g finely shredded Gouda or Parmesan cheese
- 80 g pork scratchings ground to dust

For Serving:
- 8 large round lettuce leaves
- 60 ml pico de gallo
- 20 g shredded purple cabbage
- 1 lemon, sliced
- Guacamole (optional)

Preparation Instructions
1. Preheat the air fryer to 204°C.
2. Crack the eggs into a large bowl, add the mustard, and whisk until well combined. Add the prawns and stir well to coat.
3. In a medium-sized bowl, mix together the cheese and pork scratching dust until well combined.
4. One at a time, roll the coated prawns in the pork scratching dust mixture and use your hands to press it onto each prawns. Spray the coated prawns with avocado oil and place them in the air fryer basket, leaving space between them.
5. Air fry the prawns for 9 minutes, or until cooked through and no longer translucent, flipping after 4 minutes.
6. To serve, place a lettuce leaf on a serving plate, place several prawns on top, and top with 1½ teaspoons each of pico de gallo and purple cabbage. Squeeze some lemon juice on top and serve with guacamole, if desired.
7. Store leftover prawns in an airtight container in the refrigerator for up to 3 days. Reheat in a preheated 204°C air fryer for 5 minutes, or until warmed through.

Tuna Nuggets in Hoisin Sauce

Prep time: 15 minutes

Cook Time: 5 to 7 minutes

Serves 4

Ingredients
- 120 ml hoisin sauce
- 2 tablespoons rice wine vinegar
- 2 teaspoons sesame oil
- 1 teaspoon garlic powder
- 2 teaspoons dried lemongrass
- ¼ teaspoon red pepper flakes
- ½ small onion, quartered and thinly sliced
- 230 g fresh tuna, cut into 1-inch cubes
- Cooking spray
- 560 g cooked jasmine rice

Preparation Instructions
1. Mix the hoisin sauce, vinegar, sesame oil, and seasonings together. 2. Stir in the onions and tuna nuggets.
3. Spray a baking pan with nonstick spray and pour in tuna mixture.
4. Roast at 200°C for 3 minutes. Stir gently.
5. Cook for 2 minutes and stir again, checking for doneness. Tuna should be barely cooked through, just beginning to flake and still very moist. If necessary, continue cooking and stirring in 1-minute intervals until done.
6. Serve warm over hot jasmine rice.

Cayenne Sole Cutlets

Prep time: 15 minutes

Cook Time: 10 minutes

Serves 2

Ingredients
- 1 egg
- 120 g Pecorino Romano cheese, grated
- Sea salt and white pepper, to taste
- ½ teaspoon cayenne pepper
- 1 teaspoon dried parsley flakes
- 2 sole fillets

Preparation Instructions

1. To make a breading station, whisk the egg until frothy.
2. In another bowl, mix Pecorino Romano cheese, and spices.
3. Dip the fish in the egg mixture and turn to coat evenly; then, dredge in the cracker crumb mixture, turning a couple of times to coat evenly.
4. Cook in the preheated air fryer at 200°C for 5 minutes; turn them over and cook for another 5 minutes. Enjoy!

Panko Crab Sticks with Mayo Sauce

Prep time: 5 minutes

Cook Time: 12 minutes

Serves 4

Ingredients

- Crab Sticks:
- 2 eggs
- 120 g plain flour
- 50 g panko bread crumbs
- 1 tablespoon Old Bay seasoning
- 455 g crab sticks
- Cooking spray
- Mayo Sauce:
- 115 g mayonnaise
- 1 lime, juiced
- 2 garlic cloves, minced

Preparation Instructions

1. Preheat air fryer to 200°C.
2. In a bowl, beat the eggs. In a shallow bowl, place the flour. In another shallow bowl, thoroughly combine the panko bread crumbs and old bay seasoning.
3. Dredge the crab sticks in the flour, shaking off any excess, then in the beaten eggs, finally press them in the bread crumb mixture to coat well.

4. Arrange the crab sticks in the air fryer basket and spray with cooking spray.
5. Air fry for 12 minutes until golden brown. Flip the crab sticks halfway through the Cooking Time.
6. Meanwhile, make the sauce by whisking together the mayo, lime juice, and garlic in a small bowl.
7. Serve the crab sticks with the mayo sauce on the side.

Easy Scallops

Prep time: 5 minutes

Cook Time: 4 minutes

Serves 2

Ingredients

- 12 medium sea scallops, rinsed and patted dry
- 1 teaspoon fine sea salt
- ¾ teaspoon ground black pepper, plus more for garnish
- Fresh thyme leaves, for garnish (optional)
- Avocado oil spray

Preparation Instructions

1. Preheat the air fryer to 200°C. Coat the air fryer basket with avocado oil spray.
2. Place the scallops in a medium bowl and spritz with avocado oil spray. Sprinkle the salt and pepper to season.
3. Transfer the seasoned scallops to the air fryer basket, spacing them apart. You may need to work in batches to avoid overcrowding.
4. Air fry for 4 minutes, flipping the scallops halfway through, or until the scallops are firm and reach an internal temperature of just 64°C on a meat thermometer.
5. Remove from the basket and repeat with the remaining scallops.
6. Sprinkle the pepper and thyme leaves on top for garnish, if desired. Serve immediately.

Cod Tacos with Mango Salsa

Prep time: 15 minutes

Cook Time: 17 minutes

Serves 4

Ingredients

- 1 mango, peeled and diced
- 1 small jalapeño pepper, diced
- ½ red bell pepper, diced
- ½ red onion, minced
- Pinch chopped fresh cilantro
- Juice of ½ lime
- ¼ teaspoon salt
- ¼ teaspoon ground black pepper
- 120 ml Mexican beer
- 1 egg
- 75 g cornflour
- 90 g plain flour
- ½ teaspoon ground cumin
- ¼ teaspoon chilli powder
- 455 g cod, cut into 4 pieces
- Olive oil spray
- 4 corn tortillas, or flour tortillas, at room temperature

Preparation Instructions

1. In a small bowl, stir together the mango, jalapeño, red bell pepper, red onion, cilantro, lime juice, salt, and pepper. Set aside.
2. In a medium bowl, whisk the beer and egg.
3. In another medium bowl, stir together the cornflour, flour, cumin, and chilli powder.
4. Insert the crisper plate into the basket and the basket into the unit. Preheat the unit to 192°C.
5. Dip the fish pieces into the egg mixture and in the flour mixture to coat completely.
6. Once the unit is preheated, place a baking paper liner into the basket. Place the fish on the liner in a single layer.
7. Cook for about 9 minutes, spray the fish with olive oil. Reinsert the basket to resume cooking.
8. When the cooking is complete, the fish should be golden and crispy. Place the pieces in the tortillas, top with the mango salsa, and serve.

Air Fryer Tuna Fish Cakes

Cooking Time: 12 minutes

Serves: 4

Ingredients

- 2 cans (125 g each) tuna, drained
- 50 g almond flour
- 40 g chopped onion
- 35 g chopped celery
- 40 g chopped red pepper
- 1 egg
- 1 tablespoon Dijon mustard
- 1 tablespoon lemon juice
- 1 teaspoon dried dill
- Salt and pepper, to taste
- Cooking spray

Preparation Instructions

1. In a medium bowl, mix together tuna, almond flour, chopped onion, chopped celery, chopped red pepper, egg, Dijon mustard, lemon juice, dried dill, salt, and pepper.
2. Form the mixture into 8 fish cakes. .
3. Preheat the air fryer to 190°C.
4. Spray the air fryer basket with cooking spray.
5. Place the tuna fish cakes into the air fryer basket and cook for 12 minutes, flipping halfway through.

Nutrition information per serving:

Calories: 208 Fat: 8g Saturated Fat: 1g Sodium: 326mg Carbohydrates: 5g Fibre: 2g Protein: 30g

Air Fryer Fish Tempura

Cooking Time 15 minutes

Serves: 4

Ingredients

- 4 white fish fillets, such as tilapia or cod
- 50 g oat flour
- 60 g cornflour
- 1/2 tsp. baking powder
- 1/2 tsp. salt
- 1/4 tsp. black pepper
- 120 ml cold water
- 1 large egg
- 1 tbsp. vegetable oil
- Cooking spray

Preparation Instructions

1. Preheat the air fryer to 200°C
2. In a mixing bowl, whisk together oat flour, cornflour, baking powder, salt, and black pepper.
3. In a separate mixing bowl, beat together the egg, cold water, and vegetable oil.
4. Dip each fish fillet into the wet mixture, then into the dry mixture, pressing down to coat well.
5. Place the coated fish fillets in a single layer in the air fryer basket.
6. Lightly coat the fish fillets with cooking spray.
7. Air fry the fish for 10-12 minutes or until the fish is golden brown and cooked through.
8. Serve the fish hot with your choice of dipping sauce.

Nutritional Information (per serving):

Calories: 228 Fat: 6. 7g Saturated Fat: 1. 2g
Sodium: 458mg Carbohydrate: 20g Fibre: 0. 9g
Sugars: 0. 2g Protein: 22. 6g

Air Fryer Battered Fish

Cooking Time: 10 minutes

Serves: 4

Ingredients

- 4 fillets of white fish, such as cod or haddock (120g each)
- 50g almond flour
- 50g coconut flour
- 1 tsp paprika
- 1 tsp garlic powder
- 1/2 tsp salt
- 1/4 tsp black pepper
- 1 large egg
- 120ml unsweetened almond milk
- Cooking spray

Preparation Instructions

1. Preheat the air fryer to 200°C.
2. In a bowl, whisk together the almond flour, coconut flour, paprika, garlic powder, salt, and black pepper.
3. In another bowl, beat the egg and whisk in the almond milk.
4. Dip each fillet into the egg mixture, then coat with the flour mixture.
5. Place the fillets in the air fryer basket, spray with cooking spray, and cook for 10 minutes or until the fish is cooked through and the coating is crispy.

Nutritional Information (per serving):

Calories: 227 Fat: 11g Carbohydrates: 6g Fibre: 3g
Protein: 24g Sugar: 1g Sodium: 442mg

Chapter 4: Pork, beef and lamb

Air Fryer Meatballs

Prep time: 10 minutes

Cooking Time: 12-15 minutes

Serves: 4 people

Ingredients
- 500 g minced beef or pork
- 1 large egg
- 60g breadcrumbs
- 1 small onion, finely chopped
- 2 cloves of garlic, minced
- 1 tsp dried basil
- 1 tsp dried oregano
- 1 tsp salt
- 1 tsp black pepper
- 2 tbsp olive oil
- Optional: 1/4 cup grated Parmesan cheese

Preparation Instructions
1. Preheat the air fryer to 200°C (400°F).
2. In a large mixing bowl, combine the minced beef or pork, egg, breadcrumbs, onion, garlic, basil, oregano, salt, pepper, and Parmesan cheese if using. Mix until everything is well combined.
3. Using your hands, form the mixture into golf-ball sized meatballs, making about 18-20 meatballs.
4. In a small bowl, mix together the olive oil and 1 tsp of dried basil and oregano. Brush the mixture onto the meatballs.
5. Place the meatballs in the air fryer basket in a single layer. Make sure they are not touching each other.
6. Cook for 12-15 minutes, turning them over halfway through the Cooking Time, until they are fully cooked and browned.
7. Serve the meatballs hot with your favourite sauce or in a sub roll. Enjoy!

Air Fryer BBQ Ribs

Prep time: 10 minutes

Cooking Time: 45 minutes

Serves: 4 people

Ingredients
- 1 kg pork spare ribs
- 1 tsp garlic powder
- 1 tsp onion powder
- 1 tsp smoked paprika
- 1 tsp dried oregano
- 1 tsp dried thyme
- 1 tsp salt
- 1 tsp black pepper
- 200 ml barbecue sauce

Preparation Instructions
1. In a large bowl, mix together the garlic powder, onion powder, smoked paprika, oregano, thyme, salt, and black pepper.
2. Rub the mixture evenly over the spare ribs.
3. Place the seasoned ribs in the air fryer basket and cook at 180°C (360°F) for 15 minutes.
4. Flip the ribs over and cook for an additional 15 minutes.
5. Brush the barbecue sauce over the ribs, making sure to coat both sides.
6. Cook for another 10-15 minutes, or until the internal temperature of the ribs reaches 75°C (165°F).
7. Let the ribs rest for a few minutes before cutting and serving. Enjoy your delicious BBQ ribs in the air fryer!

Air Fryer Steak

Prep time: 5 minutes

Cooking Time: 8-10 minutes

Serves: 4 people

Ingredients

- 4 (225 g) ribeye steaks
- 2 tbsp olive oil
- 1 tsp salt
- 1 tsp black pepper
- 1 tsp paprika
- 2 garlic cloves, minced
- 1 tsp dried thyme
- 1 tsp dried rosemary

Preparation Instructions

1. Preheat your air fryer to 220°C.
2. Rinse the steaks and pat them dry with paper towels.
3. In a small bowl, mix together the olive oil, salt, black pepper, paprika, garlic, thyme, and rosemary.
4. Rub the seasoning mixture onto both sides of the steaks.
5. Place the steaks in the air fryer basket in a single layer, making sure they aren't touching each other.
6. Cook for 8-10 minutes for medium-rare, flipping the steaks over halfway through, or until they reach your desired doneness.
7. Remove from the air fryer and let the steaks rest for a minute or two before serving. Enjoy!

Air Fryer Steak Jerky

Prep time: 15 minutes

Cook Time: 3-4 hours

Serves: 4-6

Ingredients

- 1 lb (450g) flank steak, sliced into thin strips
- ¼ cup (60ml) Worcestershire sauce
- ¼ cup (60ml) soy sauce
- 1 tsp (5g) onion powder
- 1 tsp (5g) garlic powder
- 1 tsp (5g) black pepper
- ¼ tsp (1g) cayenne pepper (optional)

Preparation Instructions

1. In a large bowl, whisk together Worcestershire sauce, soy sauce, onion powder, garlic powder, black pepper, and cayenne pepper (if using).
2. Add the flank steak strips to the bowl and toss to coat them evenly with the marinade.
3. Cover the bowl with plastic wrap and marinate in the refrigerator for at least 2 hours, or up to overnight.
4. Preheat your air fryer to 70°C.
5. Remove the steak strips from the marinade and pat them dry with paper towels.
6. Arrange the steak strips on the air fryer racks in a single layer, leaving some space between them.
7. Air fry the steak strips for 3-4 hours or until they are completely dried out and chewy, flipping them over every hour.
8. Once the steak jerky is done, remove them from the air fryer and let them cool completely before serving.
9. Store the jerky in an airtight container for up to 2 weeks.

Air Fryer Bacon Wrapped Avocados

Prep time: 10 minutes

Cook Time: 12 minutes

Serves: 4

Ingredients

- 2 ripe avocados, pitted and sliced into 8 wedges each
- 8 slices of bacon
- Salt and pepper, to taste
- ¼ tsp (1g) paprika
- ¼ tsp (1g) garlic powder

Preparation Instructions

1. Preheat your air fryer to 200°C.
2. Cut each slice of bacon in half lengthwise.
3. Wrap each avocado wedge with a half slice of bacon, securing it with a toothpick.
4. In a small bowl, combine the salt, pepper, paprika, and garlic powder.
5. Sprinkle the seasoning mixture over the bacon-wrapped avocado wedges.
6. Place the avocado wedges in the air fryer basket in a single layer.
7. Cook for 12 minutes or until the bacon is crispy, flipping the avocado wedges over halfway through the Cooking Time.
8. Once the avocado wedges are done, remove them from the air fryer and let them cool slightly before serving. Remove the toothpicks from the avocado wedges before serving.

Air fryer stuffed bell peppers

Prep time: 15 minutes

Cook Time: 20 minutes

Serves: 4

Ingredients

- 4 bell peppers, tops removed and seeded
- ½ lb (225g) lean ground beef
- ½ cup (80g) cooked brown rice
- ½ cup (60g) chopped onion
- ½ cup (70g) chopped mushrooms
- ½ cup (70g) chopped zucchini
- ½ cup (120ml) canned diced tomatoes, drained
- ½ tsp (2. 5ml) garlic powder
- ½ tsp (2. 5ml) dried oregano
- ½ tsp (2. 5ml) paprika
- Salt and pepper, to taste

Preparation Instructions

1. Preheat your air fryer to 180°C.
2. In a large bowl, mix together the ground beef, cooked brown rice, onion, mushrooms, zucchini, diced tomatoes, garlic powder, oregano, paprika, salt, and pepper.
3. Stuff the mixture evenly into each bell pepper.
4. Place the stuffed peppers in the air fryer basket.
5. Cook for 20 minutes, or until the bell peppers are tender and the filling is cooked through. Remove from the air fryer and let cool for a few minutes before serving.

Korean Style Beef

Prep time: 5 mins

Cook Time: 8 - 10 mins

Serves: 4

Ingredients

- 500g beef sirloin, thinly sliced
- 2 tablespoons soy sauce
- 2 tablespoons brown sugar
- 2 cloves of garlic, minced
- 1 tablespoon sesame oil
- 1 tablespoon rice vinegar
- 1/2 teaspoon red pepper flakes

Preparation Instructions

1. In a mixing bowl, combine the beef, soy sauce, brown sugar, garlic, sesame oil, rice vinegar, and red pepper flakes. Mix well.
2. Preheat your air fryer to 180C.
3. Place the beef in a single layer in the air fryer and cook for 8-10 minutes or until cooked through.

Asian Style Pork

Prep time: 5 mins

Cook Time: 8 - 10 mins

Serves: 4 - 6

Ingredients

- 500g pork tenderloin, thinly sliced

- 3 cloves of garlic, minced
- 2 tablespoons soy sauce
- 2 tablespoons hoisin sauce
- 1 tablespoon rice vinegar
- 1 tablespoon honey
- 1 teaspoon sesame oil
- 1/4 teaspoon black pepper

Preparation Instructions

1. In a mixing bowl, combine the pork, garlic, soy sauce, hoisin sauce, rice vinegar, honey, sesame oil, and pepper. Mix well.
2. Preheat your air fryer to 180C.
3. Place the pork in a single layer in the air fryer and cook for 8-10 minutes or until cooked through.

Lamb Kebabs

Prep time: 10 mins

Cook Time: 10 - 12 mins

Serves: 4 - 6

Ingredients

500g lamb, cut into 2. 5 cm cubes
- 2 cloves of garlic, minced
- 1 teaspoon ground cumin
- 1 teaspoon smoked paprika
- 1/2 teaspoon salt
- 1/4 teaspoon black pepper
- 2 tablespoons olive oil
- 1 red onion, cut into 2. 5 cm chunks
- 1 red pepper, cut into 2. 5 cm chunks
- Skewers (if using wooden skewers, soak them in water for 30 minutes before using)

Preparation Instructions

1. In a mixing bowl, combine the lamb cubes, garlic, cumin, smoked paprika, salt, pepper and olive oil. Mix well.
2. Thread the lamb cubes, onion, and bell pepper onto skewers.
3. Preheat your air fryer to 180C

4. Place the skewers in the air fryer and cook for 10-12 minutes, turning occasionally, or until the lamb is cooked through and the vegetables are slightly charred.
5. Remove the skewers from the air fryer and let them rest for a few minutes before serving.
6. You can serve this delicious lamb kebabs with some yogurt based dips, or some herbs, or with pita bread.

Mongolian-Style Beef

Prep time: 10 minutes

Cook Time: 10 minutes

Serves 4

Ingredients

- Oil, for spraying
- 30 g cornflour
- 450 g flank steak, thinly sliced
- 95 g Packed light brown sugar
- 125 g soy sauce
- 2 teaspoons toasted sesame oil
- 1 tablespoon minced garlic
- ½ teaspoon ground ginger
- 125 ml water
- Cooked white rice or ramen noodles, for serving

Preparation Instructions

1. Line the air fryer basket with baking paper and spray lightly with oil.
2. Place the cornflour in a bowl and dredge the steak until evenly coated. Shake off any excess cornflour.
3. Place the steak in the prepared basket and spray lightly with oil.
4. Roast at 200ºC for 5 minutes, flip, and cook for another 5 minutes.
5. In a small saucepan, combine the brown sugar, soy sauce, sesame oil, garlic, ginger, and water and bring to a boil over medium-high heat, stirring frequently. Remove from

the heat.

6. Transfer the meat to the sauce and toss until evenly coated. Let sit for about 5 minutes so the steak absorbs the flavours. Serve with white rice or ramen noodles.

Beef and Tomato Sauce Meatloaf

Prep time: 15 minutes

Cook Time: 25 minutes

Serves 4

Ingredients

- 680 g minced beef
- 250 g tomato sauce
- 60 g breadcrumbs
- 2 egg whites
- 60 g grated Parmesan cheese
- 1 diced onion
- 2 tablespoons chopped parsley
- 2 tablespoons minced ginger
- 2 garlic cloves, minced
- ½ teaspoon dried basil
- 1 teaspoon cayenne pepper
- Salt and ground black pepper, to taste
- Cooking spray

Preparation Instructions

1. Preheat the air fryer to 180°C. Spritz a meatloaf pan with cooking spray.
2. Combine all the Ingredients in a large bowl. Stir to mix well.
3. Pour the meat mixture in the prepared meatloaf pan and press with a spatula to make it firm.
4. Arrange the pan in the preheated air fryer and bake for 25 minutes or until the beef is well browned.
5. Serve immediately.

Sichuan Cumin Lamb

Prep time: 30 minutes

Cook Time: 10 minutes

Serves 4

Ingredients

Lamb:

- 2 tablespoons cumin seeds
- 1 teaspoon Sichuan peppercorns, or ½ teaspoon cayenne pepper
- 450 g lamb (preferably shoulder), cut into ½ by 2-inch pieces
- 2 tablespoons vegetable oil
- 1 tablespoon light soy sauce
- 1 tablespoon minced garlic
- 2 fresh red chillies, chopped
- 1 teaspoon kosher or coarse sea salt
- ¼ teaspoon sugar

For Serving:

- 2 spring onions, chopped
- Large handful of chopped fresh coriander

Preparation Instructions

1. For the lamb: In a dry skillet, toast the cumin seeds and Sichuan peppercorns (if using) over medium heat, stirring frequently, until fragrant, 1 to 2 minutes. Remove from the heat and let cool. Use a mortar and pestle to coarsely grind the toasted spices.
2. Use a fork to pierce the lamb pieces to allow the marinade to penetrate better. In a large bowl or sandwich bag, combine the toasted spices, vegetable oil, soy sauce, garlic, chillies, salt, and sugar. Add the lamb to the bag. Seal and massage to coat. Marinate at room temperature for 30 minutes.
3. Place the lamb in a single layer in the air fryer basket. Set the air fryer to 176°C for 10 minutes. Use a meat thermometer to ensure the lamb has reached an internal temperature of 64°C (medium-rare).
4. Transfer the lamb to a serving bowl. Stir in the spring onions and coriander and serve.

Lamb Chops with Horseradish Sauce

Prep time: 30 minutes

Cook Time: 13 minutes

Serves 4

Ingredients

Lamb:
- 4 lamb loin chops
- 2 tablespoons vegetable oil
- 1 clove garlic, minced
- ½ teaspoon coarse or flaky salt
- ½ teaspoon black pepper

Horseradish Cream Sauce:
- 120 ml mayonnaise
- 1 tablespoon Dijon mustard
- 1 to 1½ tablespoons grated horseradish
- 2 teaspoons sugar
- Vegetable oil spray

Preparation Instructions

1. For the lamb: Brush the lamb chops with the oil, rub with the garlic, and sprinkle with the salt and pepper. Marinate at room temperature for 30 minutes.
2. Meanwhile, for the sauce: In a medium bowl, combine the mayonnaise, mustard, horseradish, and sugar. Stir until well combined. Set aside half of the sauce for serving.
3. Spray the air fryer basket with vegetable oil spray and place the chops in the basket. Set the air fryer to 164°C for 10 minutes, turning the chops halfway through the Cooking Time.
4. Remove the chops from the air fryer and add to the bowl with the horseradish sauce, turning to coat with the sauce. Place the chops back in the air fryer basket. Set the air fryer to 204°C for 3 minutes. Use a meat thermometer to ensure the meat has reached an internal temperature of 64°C (for medium-rare).
5. Serve the chops with the reserved horseradish sauce.

Pork and Tricolor Vegetables Kebabs

Prep time: 1 hour 20 minutes

Cook Time: 8 minutes per batch

Serves 4

Ingredients

- For the Pork:
- 450 g pork steak, cut in cubes
- 1 tablespoon white wine vinegar
- 3 tablespoons steak sauce or brown sauce
- 60 ml soy sauce
- 1 teaspoon powdered chili
- 1 teaspoon red chili flakes
- 2 teaspoons smoked paprika
- 1 teaspoon garlic salt
- For the Vegetable:
- 1 courgette, cut in cubes
- 1 butternut squash, deseeded and cut in cubes
- 1 red pepper, cut in cubes
- 1 green pepper, cut in cubes
- Salt and ground black pepper, to taste
- Cooking spray
- Special Equipment:
- 4 bamboo skewers, soaked in water for at least 30 minutes

Preparation Instructions

1. Combine the Ingredients for the pork in a large bowl. Press the pork to dunk in the marinade. Wrap the bowl in plastic and refrigerate for at least an hour.
2. Preheat the air fryer to 188°C and spritz with cooking spray.
3. Remove the pork from the marinade and run the skewers through the pork and vegetables alternately. Sprinkle with salt and pepper to taste.
4. Arrange the skewers in the preheated air fryer and spritz with cooking spray. Air fry for 8 minutes or until the pork is browned and the

vegetables are lightly charred and tender. Flip the skewers halfway through. You may need to work in batches to avoid overcrowding.

5. Serve immediately.

Chuck Kebab with Rocket

Prep time: 30 minutes

Cook Time: 25 minutes

Serves 4

Ingredients

- 120 ml leeks, chopped
- 2 garlic cloves, smashed
- 900 g beef mince
- Salt, to taste
- ¼ teaspoon ground black pepper, or more to taste
- 1 teaspoon cayenne pepper
- ½ teaspoon ground sumac
- 3 saffron threads
- 2 tablespoons loosely packed fresh flat-leaf parsley leaves
- 4 tablespoons tahini sauce
- 110 g baby rocket
- 1 tomato, cut into slices

Preparation Instructions

1. In a bowl, mix the chopped leeks, garlic, beef mince, and spices; knead with your hands until everything is well incorporated.

2. Now, mound the beef mixture around a wooden skewer into a pointed-ended sausage.

3. Cook in the preheated air fryer at 182ºC for 25 minutes. Serve your kebab with the tahini sauce, baby rocket and tomato. Enjoy!

Greek Stuffed Fillet

Prep time: 10 minutes

Cook Time: 10 minutes

Serves 4

Ingredients

- 680 g venison or beef fillet, pounded to ¼ inch thick
- 3 teaspoons fine sea salt
- 1 teaspoon ground black pepper
- 60 g creamy goat cheese
- 120 ml crumbled feta cheese (about 60 g)
- 60 ml finely chopped onions
- 2 cloves garlic, minced
- For Garnish

Serving (Optional):
- Yellow
- American mustard
- Halved cherry tomatoes
- Extra-virgin olive oil
- Sprigs of fresh rosemary
- Lavender flowers

Preparation Instructions

1. Spray the air fryer basket with avocado oil. Preheat the air fryer to 204ºC.

2. Season the fillet on all sides with salt and pepper.

3. In a medium-sized mixing bowl, combine the goat cheese, feta, onions, and garlic. Place the mixture in the centre of the tenderloin. Starting at the end closest to you, tightly roll the tenderloin like a jelly roll. Tie the rolled tenderloin tightly with kitchen twine.

4. Place the meat in the air fryer basket and air fry for 5 minutes. Flip the meat over and cook for another 5 minutes, or until the internal temperature reaches 57ºC for medium-rare.

5. To serve, smear a line of yellow mustard on a platter, then place the meat next to it and add halved cherry tomatoes on the side, if desired. Drizzle with olive oil and garnish with rosemary sprigs and lavender flowers, if desired.

6. Best served fresh. Store leftovers in an airtight container in the fridge for 3 days. Reheat in a preheated 176ºC air fryer for 4

minutes, or until heated through.

Stuffed Beef Fillet with Feta Cheese

Prep time: 10 minutes

Cook Time: 10 minutes

Serves 4

Ingredients

- 680 g beef fillet, pounded to ¼ inch thick
- 3 teaspoons sea salt
- 1 teaspoon ground black pepper
- 60 g creamy goat cheese
- 120 ml crumbled feta cheese
- 60 ml finely chopped onions
- 2 cloves garlic, minced
- Cooking spray

Preparation Instructions

1. Preheat the air fryer to 204°C. Spritz the air fryer basket with cooking spray.
2. Unfold the beef on a clean work surface. Rub the salt and pepper all over the beef to season.
3. Make the filling for the stuffed beef fillet: Combine the goat cheese, feta, onions, and garlic in a medium bowl. Stir until well blended.
4. Spoon the mixture in the centre of the fillet. Roll the fillet up tightly like rolling a burrito and use some kitchen twine to tie the fillet.
5. Arrange the fillet in the air fryer basket and air fry for 10 minutes, flipping the fillet halfway through to ensure even cooking, or until an instant-read thermometer inserted in the centre of the fillet registers 57°C for medium-rare.
6. Transfer to a platter and serve immediately.

Chinese-Inspired Spareribs

Prep time: 30 minutes

Cook Time: 8 minutes

Serves 4

Ingredients

- Oil, for spraying
- 340 g boneless pork spareribs, cut into 3-inch-long pieces
- 235 ml soy sauce
- 180 ml sugar
- 120 ml beef or chicken stock
- 60 ml honey
- 2 tablespoons minced garlic
- 1 teaspoon ground ginger
- 2 drops red food colouring (optional)

Preparation Instructions

1. Line the air fryer basket with parchment and spray lightly with oil.
2. Combine the ribs, soy sauce, sugar, beef stock, honey, garlic, ginger, and food colouring (if using) in a large zip-top plastic bag, seal, and shake well until completely coated.
3. Refrigerate for at least 30 minutes.
4. Place the ribs in the prepared basket. Air fry at 192°C for 8 minutes, or until the internal temperature reaches 74°C.

Bacon and Pepper Sandwiches

Prep time: 15 minutes

Cook Time: 7 minutes

Serves 4

Ingredients

- 80 ml spicy barbecue sauce
- 2 tablespoons honey
- 8 slices pre-cooked bacon, cut into thirds
- 1 red pepper, sliced
- 1 yellow pepper, sliced
- 3 pitta pockets, cut in half
- 300 ml torn butterhead lettuce leaves
- 2 tomatoes, sliced

Preparation Instructions

1. In a small bowl, combine the barbecue sauce and the honey.

2. Brush this mixture lightly onto the bacon slices and the red and yellow pepper slices.
3. Put the peppers into the air fryer basket and air fry at 176°C for 4 minutes. Then shake the basket, add the bacon, and air fry for 2 minutes or until the bacon is browned and the peppers are tender.
4. Fill the pitta halves with the bacon, peppers, any remaining barbecue sauce, lettuce, and tomatoes, and serve immediately.

Korean Flavour Beef and Onion Tacos

Prep time: 1 hour 15 minutes

Cook Time: 12 minutes

Serves 6

Ingredients
- 2 tablespoons gochujang chilli sauce
- 1 tablespoon soy sauce
- 2 tablespoons sesame seeds
- 2 teaspoons minced fresh ginger
- 2 cloves garlic, minced
- 2 tablespoons toasted sesame oil
- 2 teaspoons sugar
- ½ teaspoon rock salt
- 680 g thinly sliced braising steak
- 1 medium red onion, sliced
- 6 corn tortillas, warmed
- 60 ml chopped fresh coriander
- 120 ml kimchi
- 120 ml chopped spring onions

Preparation Instructions
1. Combine the gochujang, soy sauce, sesame seeds, ginger, garlic, sesame oil, sugar, and salt in a large bowl. Stir to mix well.
2. Dunk the braising steak in the large bowl. Press to submerge, then wrap the bowl in plastic and refrigerate to marinate for at least 1 hour.
3. Preheat the air fryer to 204°C.

4. Remove the braising steak from the marinade and transfer to the preheated air fryer basket.
5. Add the onion and air fry for 12 minutes or until well browned. Shake the basket halfway through.
6. Unfold the tortillas on a clean work surface, then divide the fried beef and onion on the tortillas. Spread the coriander, kimchi, and spring onions on top.
7. Serve immediately.

Barbecue Pulled Pork Sandwiches

Prep time: 15 minutes

Cook Time: 30 minutes

Serves 4

Ingredients
- 350 ml prepared barbecue sauce
- 2 tablespoons distilled white vinegar
- 2 tablespoons light brown sugar
- 1 tablespoon minced garlic
- 1 teaspoon hot sauce
- 900 g pork shoulder roast
- 1 to 2 tablespoons oil
- 4 sandwich buns

Preparation Instructions
1. In a medium bowl, stir together the barbecue sauce, vinegar, brown sugar, garlic, and hot sauce.
2. Preheat the air fryer to 182°C. Line the air fryer basket with parchment paper and spritz it with oil.
3. Place the pork on the parchment and baste it with a thick layer of sauce. Cook for 5 minutes. Flip the pork and baste with sauce.
4. Repeat 3 more times for a total of 20 minutes of Cook Time, ending with basting.
5. Increase the air fryer temperature to 200°C. Cook the pork for 5 minutes. Flip and baste. Cook for 5 minutes more. Flip and baste. Let

sit for 5 minutes before pulling the pork into 1-inch pieces. Transfer to a bowl and toss the pork with the remaining sauce.

6. Serve on buns.

Caraway Crusted Beef Steaks

Prep time: 5 minutes

Cook Time: 10 minutes

Serves 4

Ingredients

- 4 beef steaks
- 2 teaspoons caraway seeds
- 2 teaspoons garlic powder
- Sea salt and cayenne pepper, to taste
- 1 tablespoon melted butter
- 80 ml almond flour
- 2 eggs, beaten

Preparation Instructions

1. Preheat the air fryer to 179°C.
2. Add the beef steaks to a large bowl and toss with the caraway seeds, garlic powder, salt and pepper until well coated.
3. Stir together the melted butter and almond flour in a bowl. Whisk the eggs in a different bowl.
4. Dredge the seasoned steaks in the eggs, then dip in the almond and butter mixture.
5. Arrange the coated steaks in the air fryer basket. Air fryer for 10 minutes, or until the internal temperature of the beef steaks reaches at least 64°C on a meat thermometer. Flip the steaks once halfway through to ensure even cooking.
6. Transfer the steaks to plates. Let cool for 5 minutes and serve hot.

Cinnamon-Beef Kofta

Prep time: 10 minutes

Cook Time: 13 minutes per batch

Makes 12 koftas

Ingredients

- 680 g lean beef mince
- 1 teaspoon onion granules
- ¾ teaspoon ground cinnamon
- ¾ teaspoon ground dried turmeric
- 1 teaspoon ground cumin
- ¾ teaspoon salt
- ¼ teaspoon cayenne
- 12 (3½- to 4-inch-long) cinnamon sticks
- Cooking spray

Preparation Instructions

1. Preheat the air fryer to 192°C. Spritz the air fryer basket with cooking spray.
2. Combine all the Ingredients, except for the cinnamon sticks, in a large bowl. Toss to mix well.
3. Divide and shape the mixture into 12 balls, then wrap each ball around each cinnamon stick and leave a quarter of the length uncovered.
4. Arrange the beef-cinnamon sticks in the preheated air fryer and spritz with cooking spray. Work in batches to avoid overcrowding.
5. Air fry for 13 minutes or until the beef is browned. Flip the sticks halfway through.
6. Serve immediately.

Mushroom in Bacon-Wrapped Filets Mignons

Prep time: 10 minutes

Cook Time: 13 minutes per batch

Serves 8

Ingredients

- 30 g dried porcini mushrooms
- ½ teaspoon granulated white sugar
- ½ teaspoon salt
- ½ teaspoon ground white pepper
- 8 (110 g) filets mignons or beef fillet steaks
- 8 thin-cut bacon strips

Preparation Instructions

1. Preheat the air fryer to 204°C.

2. Put the mushrooms, sugar, salt, and white pepper in a spice grinder and grind to combine.

3. On a clean work surface, rub the fillet mignons with the mushroom mixture, then wrap each fillet with a bacon strip. Secure with toothpicks if necessary.

4. Arrange the bacon-wrapped fillets mignons in the preheated air fryer basket, seam side down. Work in batches to avoid overcrowding.

5. Air fry for 13 minutes or until medium rare. Flip the fillets halfway through.

6. Serve immediately.

Air Fryer Pork Chops

Cooking Time: 15 minutes

Serves 2

Ingredients

- 2 boneless pork chops
- 1/2 tsp smoked paprika
- 1/2 tsp garlic powder
- 1/2 tsp onion powder
- Salt and pepper, to taste

Preparation Instructions

1. Preheat the air fryer to 200°C.

2. In a small bowl, mix together the smoked paprika, garlic powder, onion powder, salt, and pepper.

3. Season the pork chops with the spice mixture, making sure to coat both sides evenly.

4. Place the pork chops in the air fryer basket and cook for 10-15 minutes, flipping halfway through, until the internal temperature reaches 63°C.

Air Fryer Pork Tenderloin

Cooking Time: 20 minutes

Serves 4

Ingredients

- 455 g pork tenderloin
- 2 tbsp olive oil
- 1/2 tsp dried thyme
- 1/2 tsp dried rosemary
- 1/2 tsp garlic powder
- Salt and pepper, to taste

Preparation Instructions

1. Preheat the air fryer to 200°C.

2. Rub the pork tenderloin with olive oil.

3. Mix together the dried thyme, dried rosemary, garlic powder, salt, and pepper in a small bowl.

4. Rub the spice mixture over the pork tenderloin, making sure to coat all sides evenly.

5. Place the pork tenderloin in the air fryer basket and cook for 20 minutes, flipping halfway through, until the internal temperature reaches 63°C.

Air Fryer Pork Belly Bites

Cooking Time: 20 minutes

Serves 4

Ingredients

- 455 g pork belly, cut into bite-sized pieces
- 1 tbsp olive oil
- 1/2 tsp smoked paprika
- 1/2 tsp garlic powder
- 1/2 tsp onion powder
- Salt and pepper, to taste

Preparation Instructions

1. Preheat the air fryer to 200°C.

2. In a small bowl, mix together the smoked paprika, garlic powder, onion powder, salt, and pepper.

3. Toss the pork belly pieces with olive oil and the spice mixture, making sure to coat all pieces evenly.

4. Place the pork belly pieces in the air fryer basket and cook for 15-20 minutes, shaking the basket halfway through, until crispy and cooked through.

Chapter 5: Vegetables and Sides

Air Fryer Tofu Stir Fry with Vegetables

Prep time: 10 minutes

Cooking Time: 15-20 minutes

Serves: 4 people

Ingredients

- 450 g extra firm tofu, drained and cut into bite-sized cubes
- 2 tbsp cornstarch
- 1 tsp salt
- 1 tsp black pepper
- 2 tbsp vegetable oil
- 2 bell peppers, sliced
- 1 onion, sliced
- 2 cloves of garlic, minced
- 200 g broccoli florets
- 2 tbsp soy sauce
- 2 tbsp hoisin sauce
- 1 tsp sesame oil

Preparation Instructions

1. In a large bowl, mix together the tofu, cornstarch, salt, and pepper until well coated.
2. Preheat the air fryer to 400°F (200°C).
3. Place the tofu in a single layer in the air fryer basket. Cook for 10-15 minutes, flipping the tofu halfway through cooking, or until crispy and golden brown. Remove from the air fryer and set aside.
4. In a large wok or frying pan, heat the vegetable oil over high heat. Add the bell peppers, onion, garlic, and broccoli, and stir-fry for 2-3 minutes or until the vegetables are tender.
5. Add the crispy tofu to the pan, along with the soy sauce, hoisin sauce, and sesame oil. Stir-fry for an additional 2-3 minutes or until

the sauce is well combined and the tofu is heated through.
6. Serve hot over rice or noodles. Enjoy!

Air Fryer Sweet Potato Falafel with Tahini Sauce

Prep time: 10 minutes

Cooking Time: 15-20 minutes

Serves: 4 people

Ingredients

- 500 g sweet potatoes, peeled and grated
- 400 g chickpeas, drained and rinsed
- 1 onion, chopped
- 2 cloves of garlic, minced
- 2 tbsp chickpea flour
- 2 tbsp olive oil
- 1 tsp cumin
- 1 tsp coriander
- 1 tsp paprika
- Salt and pepper, to taste

For Tahini Sauce:
- 75 ml tahini
- 2 tbsp lemon juice
- 1 clove of garlic, minced
- 2 tbsp water
- Salt and pepper, to taste

Preparation Instructions

1. In a large bowl, mix together the grated sweet potatoes, chickpeas, onion, garlic, chickpea flour, olive oil, cumin, coriander, paprika, salt, and pepper until well combined.
2. Preheat the air fryer to 400°F (200°C).
3. Shape the mixture into small patties, about 2-3 cm in diameter.
4. Place the patties in the air fryer basket in a single layer, making sure not to overcrowd.

5. Cook for 15-20 minutes, flipping the patties halfway through cooking, or until they are crispy and golden brown.
6. Tahini Sauce:
7. In a small bowl, whisk together the tahini, lemon juice, garlic, water, salt, and pepper until smooth.
8. Serve the sweet potato falafel with the tahini sauce on the side for dipping. Enjoy!

Air Fryer Portobello Mushroom Burgers

Prep time: 10 minutes

Cooking Time: 12-15 minutes

Serves: 4 people

Ingredients
- 4 large portobello mushrooms, stems removed
- 1 tbsp olive oil
- 2 cloves of garlic, minced
- 1 tsp dried thyme
- Salt and pepper, to taste
- 4 hamburger buns
- 4 slices of cheddar cheese
- 4 tbsp mayonnaise
- 4 lettuce leaves
- 4 slices of tomato

Preparation Instructions
1. Preheat the air fryer to 400°F (200°C).
2. In a small bowl, mix together the olive oil, garlic, thyme, salt, and pepper.
3. Brush both sides of the portobello mushrooms with the olive oil mixture.
4. Place the mushrooms in the air fryer basket, gill side up, in a single layer.
5. Cook for 10-12 minutes, or until tender and juicy.
6. Toast the hamburger buns in the air fryer for 2-3 minutes, or until lightly toasted.
7. Assemble the burgers by spreading mayonnaise on the bottom bun, followed by a lettuce leaf, tomato slice, portobello mushroom, and a slice of cheddar cheese.
8. Serve hot and enjoy!

Air Fryer Roasted Balsamic Brussels Sprouts

Prep time: 10 minutes

Cook Time: 15 minutes

Serves: 4

Ingredients
- 500g Brussels sprouts, trimmed and halved
- 1 tbsp (15ml) olive oil
- 1 tbsp (15ml) balsamic vinegar
- 1/2 tsp (2. 5g) garlic powder
- 1/2 tsp (0. 5g) dried thyme
- Salt and pepper, to taste

Preparation Instructions
1. Preheat your air fryer to 200°C.
2. In a large bowl, combine the Brussels sprouts, olive oil, balsamic vinegar, garlic powder, thyme, salt, and pepper.
3. Toss the Brussels sprouts to coat them evenly with the mixture.
4. Transfer the Brussels sprouts to the air fryer basket and cook for 12-15 minutes or until they are tender and slightly charred.
5. Serve the roasted Brussels sprouts as a side dish or snack.

Air Fryer Kung Pao Brussels Sprouts

Prep time: 10 minutes

Cook Time: 15 minutes

Serves: 4

Ingredients
- 500g Brussels sprouts, trimmed and halved

- 2 tbsp (30ml) soy sauce
- 1 tbsp (15ml) honey
- 1 tbsp (15ml) rice vinegar
- 1 tbsp (15ml) vegetable oil
- 1 tbsp (15ml) sesame oil
- ½ tsp (2. 5g) garlic powder
- ½ tsp (1g) ginger powder
- ½ tsp (2g) crushed red pepper flakes
- ¼ cup (30g) roasted peanuts, chopped
- 2 green onions, sliced

Preparation Instructions

1. Preheat your air fryer to 200°C.
2. In a large bowl, combine the soy sauce, honey, rice vinegar, vegetable oil, sesame oil, garlic powder, ginger powder, and crushed red pepper flakes.
3. Add the Brussels sprouts to the bowl and toss to coat them evenly with the sauce mixture.
4. Transfer the Brussels sprouts to the air fryer basket and cook for 12-15 minutes or until they are tender and slightly charred.
5. Once the Brussels sprouts are cooked, transfer them to a serving dish and sprinkle with chopped peanuts and sliced green onions.
6. Serve the Kung Pao Brussels sprouts as a side dish or main course.

Air Fryer Roasted Carrot Salad with Feta and Mint

Prep time: 10 minutes

Cook Time: 20 minutes

Serves: 4

Ingredients

- 500g carrots, peeled and sliced into ½ inch pieces
- 1 tbsp (15ml) olive oil
- Salt and pepper, to taste
- ¼ cup (35g) crumbled feta cheese
- 2 tbsp (4g) chopped fresh mint leaves

- For the dressing:
- ¼ cup (60ml) olive oil
- 2 tbsp (30ml) balsamic vinegar
- 1 tbsp (15ml) honey
- ½ tsp (2. 5g) Dijon mustard
- Salt and pepper, to taste

Preparation Instructions

1. Preheat your air fryer to 200°C.
2. In a large bowl, toss the carrot slices with olive oil, salt, and pepper.
3. Transfer the carrots to the air fryer basket and cook for 15-20 minutes or until they are tender and slightly browned.
4. While the carrots are cooking, whisk together the olive oil, balsamic vinegar, honey, Dijon mustard, salt, and pepper in a small bowl to make the dressing.
5. Once the carrots are done, transfer them to a large serving bowl and drizzle the dressing over the top.
6. Sprinkle the crumbled feta cheese and chopped mint leaves over the carrots and toss gently to combine.
7. Serve the roasted carrot salad warm or at room temperature.

Cauliflower Steaks

Prep time: 5 mins

Cook Time: 15 - 20 mins

Serves: 4

Ingredients

- 1 head of cauliflower, cut into 2 cm steaks
- 2 tablespoons of olive oil
- 1 teaspoon of cumin
- 1 teaspoon of smoked paprika
- Salt and pepper, to taste

Preparation Instructions

1. Preheat the air fryer to 180 °C.

2. In a small bowl, mix together the olive oil, cumin, smoked paprika, salt and pepper.
3. Brush the cauliflower steaks with the mixture and place them in the air fryer.
4. Cook for 15-20 minutes, or until tender and golden brown, turning halfway through.
5. Remove from the air fryer and serve as a main dish.

Parmesan Aubergine

Prep time: 30 mins

Cook Time: 20 mins

Serves: 4

Ingredients
- 2 aubergines, sliced into ½ cm rounds
- Salt and pepper, to taste
- 125 g flour
- 2 eggs, beaten
- 100 g breadcrumbs
- 100 g grated Parmesan cheese
- 240 g marinara sauce
- 120 g shredded mozzarella cheese

Preparation Instructions
1. Preheat the air fryer to 180 °C.
2. Place the aubergine slices on a baking sheet and sprinkle with salt and pepper. Allow to sit for 30 minutes to release excess moisture.
3. Place the flour in a shallow dish, the beaten eggs in a second dish, and the breadcrumbs in a third dish.
4. Dip the aubergine slices in flour, then eggs, and finally in breadcrumbs, pressing the breadcrumbs onto the aubergine to make sure they stick.
5. Place the breaded aubergine slices in the air fryer and cook for 8-10 minutes or until golden brown.
6. Remove from the air fryer and drain on a paper towel.

7. In a baking dish, layer the cooked aubergine slices, marinara sauce, Parmesan cheese and mozzarella cheese.
8. Place the dish back in the air fryer and cook for another 5-7 minutes or until the cheese is melted and bubbly.
9. Remove from the air fryer and let it sit for a few minutes before serving.

Vegetable Kebabs

Prep time: 10 mins

Cook Time: 10 mins

Serves: 4

Ingredients
- 250g mixed vegetables (such as peppers, onions, mushrooms, and cherry tomatoes), cut into bite-size pieces
- 2 tablespoons of olive oil
- 1 teaspoon of dried oregano
- 1 teaspoon of dried thyme
- Salt and pepper, to taste

Preparation Instructions
1. Preheat the air fryer to 180 °C.
2. In a small bowl, mix together the olive oil, oregano, thyme, salt, and pepper.
3. Thread the vegetables onto skewers, alternating between different types of vegetables.
4. Brush the skewers with the olive oil mixture.
5. Place the skewers in the air fryer.
6. Cook for 8-10 minutes, or until the vegetables are tender and slightly charred, turning halfway through.

Green Tomato Salad

Prep time: 10 minutes

Cook Time: 8 to 10 minutes

Serves 4

Ingredients

- 4 green tomatoes
- ½ teaspoon salt
- 1 large egg, lightly beaten
- 60 g peanut flour
- 1 tablespoon Creole seasoning
- 1 (140 g) bag rocket
- Buttermilk Dressing:
- 250 g mayonnaise
- 125 g sour cream
- 2 teaspoons fresh lemon juice
- 2 tablespoons finely chopped fresh parsley
- 1 teaspoon dried dill
- 1 teaspoon dried chives
- ½ teaspoon salt
- ½ teaspoon garlic powder
- ½ teaspoon onion powder

Preparation Instructions

1. Preheat the air fryer to 204°C.
2. Slice the tomatoes into ½-inch slices and sprinkle with the salt. Let sit for 5 to 10 minutes.
3. Place the egg in a small shallow bowl. In another small shallow bowl, combine the peanut flour and Creole seasoning. Dip each tomato slice into the egg wash, then dip into the peanut flour mixture, turning to coat evenly.
4. Working in batches if necessary, arrange the tomato slices in a single layer in the air fryer basket and spray both sides lightly with olive oil. Air fry until browned and crisp, 8 to 10 minutes.
5. To make the buttermilk dressing: In a small bowl, whisk together the mayonnaise, sour cream, lemon juice, parsley, dill, chives, salt, garlic powder, and onion powder.
6. Serve the tomato slices on top of a bed of the arugula with the dressing on the side.

Hasselback Potatoes with Chive Pesto

Prep time: 10 minutes

Cook Time: 40 minutes

Serves 2

Ingredients

- 2 medium russet potatoes
- 5 tablespoons olive oil
- Kosher or coarse sea salt and freshly ground black pepper, to taste
- 5 g roughly chopped fresh chives
- 2 tablespoons packed fresh flat-leaf parsley leaves
- 1 tablespoon chopped walnuts
- 1 tablespoon grated Parmesan cheese
- 1 teaspoon fresh lemon juice
- 1 small garlic clove, peeled
- 60 g sour cream

Preparation Instructions

1. Place the potatoes on a cutting board and lay a chopstick or thin-handled wooden spoon to the side of each potato. Thinly slice the potatoes crosswise, letting the chopstick or spoon handle stop the blade of your knife, and stop 1/2 inch short of each end of the potato. Rub the potatoes with 1 tablespoon of the olive oil and season with salt and pepper.
2. Place the potatoes, cut-side up, in the air fryer and airfryer at 192°C until golden brown and crisp on the outside and tender inside, about 40 minutes, drizzling the insides with 1 tablespoon more olive oil and seasoning with more salt and pepper halfway through.
3. Meanwhile, in a small blender or food processor, combine the remaining 3 tablespoons olive oil, the chives, parsley,

walnuts, Parmesan, lemon juice, and garlic and purée until smooth. Season the chive pesto with salt and pepper.

4. Remove the potatoes from the air fryer and transfer to plates. Drizzle the potatoes with the pesto, letting it drip down into the grooves, then dollop each with sour cream and serve hot.

Asparagus Fries

Prep time: 15 minutes

Cook Time: 5 to 7 minutes per batch

Serves 4

Ingredients

- 340 g fresh asparagus spears with tough ends trimmed off
- 2 egg whites
- 60 ml water
- 95 g Panko bread crumbs
- 60 g grated Parmesan cheese, plus 2 tablespoons
- ¼ teaspoon salt
- Oil for misting or cooking spray

Preparation Instructions

1. Preheat the air fryer to 200ºC.
2. In a shallow dish, beat egg whites and water until slightly foamy.
3. In another shallow dish, combine panko, Parmesan, and salt.
4. Dip asparagus spears in egg, then roll in crumbs. Spray with oil or cooking spray.
5. Place a layer of asparagus in the air fryer basket, leaving just a little space in between each spear. Stack another layer on top, crosswise. Air fry at 200ºC for 5 to 7 minutes, until crispy and golden brown.
6. Repeat to cook remaining asparagus.

Polenta Casserole

Prep time: 5 minutes

Cook Time: 28 to 30 minutes

Serves 4

Ingredients

- 10 fresh asparagus spears, cut into 1-inch pieces
- 320 g cooked polenta, cooled to room temperature
- 1 egg, beaten
- 2 teaspoons Worcestershire sauce
- ½ teaspoon garlic powder
- ¼ teaspoon salt
- 2 slices emmental cheese (about 40 g)
- Oil for misting or cooking spray

Preparation Instructions

1. Mist asparagus spears with oil and air fry at 200ºC for 5 minutes, until crisp-tender.
2. In a medium bowl, mix together the grits, egg, Worcestershire, garlic powder, and salt.
3. Spoon half of the polenta mixture into a baking pan and top with asparagus.
4. Tear cheese slices into pieces and layer evenly on top of asparagus.
5. Top with remaining polenta.
6. Bake at 180ºC for 23 to 25 minutes. The casserole will rise a little as it cooks. When done, the top will have browned lightly with just a hint of crispiness.

Zesty Fried Asparagus

Prep time: 3 minutes

Cook Time: 10 minutes

Serves 4

Ingredients

- Oil, for spraying
- 10 to 12 spears asparagus, trimmed
- 2 tablespoons olive oil
- 1 tablespoon garlic powder

- 1 teaspoon chili powder
- ½ teaspoon ground cumin
- ¼ teaspoon salt

Preparation Instructions

1. Line the air fryer basket with parchment and spray lightly with oil.
2. If the asparagus are too long to fit easily in the air fryer, cut them in half.
3. Place the asparagus, olive oil, garlic, chilli powder, cumin, and salt in a zip-top plastic bag, seal, and toss until evenly coated.
4. Place the asparagus in the prepared basket.
5. Roast at 200°C for 5 minutes, flip, and cook for another 5 minutes, or until bright green and firm but tender.

Curried Fruit

Prep time: 10 minutes

Cook Time: 20 minutes

Serves 6 to 8

Ingredients

- 210 g cubed fresh pineapple
- 200 g cubed fresh pear (firm, not overly ripe)
- 230 g frozen peaches, thawed
- 425 g can dark, sweet, pitted cherries with juice
- 2 tablespoons brown sugar
- 1 teaspoon curry powder

Preparation Instructions

1. Combine all Ingredients in a large bowl. Stir gently to mix in the sugar and curry.
2. Pour into a baking pan and bake at 180°C for 10 minutes.
3. Stir fruit and cook for 10 more minutes.
4. Serve hot.

Vegetable Burgers

Prep time: 10 minutes

Cook Time: 12 minutes

Serves 4

Ingredients

- 227 g cremini or chestnut mushrooms
- 2 large egg yolks
- ½ medium courgette, trimmed and chopped
- 60 ml peeled and chopped brown onion
- 1 clove garlic, peeled and finely minced
- ½ teaspoon salt
- ¼ teaspoon ground black pepper

Preparation Instructions

1. Place all Ingredients into a food processor and pulse twenty times until finely chopped and combined.
2. Separate mixture into four equal sections and press each into a burger shape.
3. Place burgers into an ungreased air fryer basket. Adjust the temperature to 192°C and air fry for 12 minutes, turning burgers halfway through cooking. Burgers will be browned and firm when done.
4. Place burgers on a large plate and let cool for 5 minutes before serving.

Pesto Vegetable Skewers

Prep time: 30 minutes

Cook Time: 8 minutes

Makes 8 skewers

Ingredients

- 1 medium courgette, trimmed and cut into ½-inch slices
- ½ medium brown onion, peeled and cut into 1-inch squares
- 1 medium red pepper, seeded and cut into 1-inch squares

- 16 whole cremini or chestnut mushrooms
- 80 ml basil pesto
- ½ teaspoon salt
- ¼ teaspoon ground black pepper

Preparation Instructions

1. Divide courgette slices, onion, and pepper into eight even portions.
2. Place on 6-inch skewers for a total of eight kebabs.
3. Add 2 mushrooms to each skewer and brush kebabs generously with pesto. . Sprinkle each kebab with salt and black pepper on all sides, then place into an ungreased air fryer basket.
4. Adjust the temperature to 192°C and air fry for 8 minutes, turning kebabs halfway through cooking.
5. Vegetables will be browned at the edges and tender-crisp when done. Serve warm.

Potato and Broccoli with Tofu Scramble

Prep time: 15 minutes

Cook Time: 30 minutes

Serves 3

Ingredients

- 600 ml chopped red potato
- 2 tablespoons olive oil, divided
- 1 block tofu, chopped finely
- 2 tablespoons tamari
- 1 teaspoon turmeric powder
- ½ teaspoon onion powder
- ½ teaspoon garlic powder
- 120 ml chopped onion
- 1 L broccoli florets

Preparation Instructions

1. Preheat the air fryer to 204°C.
2. Toss together the potatoes and 1 tablespoon

of the olive oil.

3. Air fry the potatoes in a baking dish for 15 minutes, shaking once during the Cooking Time to ensure they fry evenly.
4. Combine the tofu, the remaining 1 tablespoon of the olive oil, turmeric, onion powder, tamari, and garlic powder together, stirring in the onions, followed by the broccoli.
5. Top the potatoes with the tofu mixture and air fry for an additional 15 minutes. Serve warm.

Lush Vegetable Salad

Prep time: 15 minutes

Cook Time: 10 minutes

Serves 4

Ingredients

- 6 plum tomatoes, halved
- 2 large red onions, sliced
- 4 long red pepper, sliced
- 2 yellow pepper, sliced
- 6 cloves garlic, crushed
- 1 tablespoon extra-virgin olive oil
- 1 teaspoon paprika
- ½ lemon, juiced
- Salt and ground black pepper, to taste
- 1 tablespoon baby capers

Preparation Instructions

1. Preheat the air fryer to 220°C.
2. Put the tomatoes, onions, peppers, and garlic in a large bowl and cover with the extra-virgin olive oil, paprika, and lemon juice. Sprinkle it with salt and pepper as desired.
3. Line the inside of the air fryer basket with aluminium foil. Put the vegetables inside and air fry for 10 minutes, ensuring the edges turn brown.
4. Serve in a salad bowl with the baby capers.

Fig, Chickpea, and Rocket Salad

Prep time: 15 minutes

Cook Time: 20 minutes

Serves 4

Ingredients

- 8 fresh figs, halved
- 250 g cooked chickpeas
- 1 teaspoon crushed roasted cumin seeds
- 4 tablespoons balsamic vinegar
- 2 tablespoons extra-virgin olive oil, plus more for greasing
- Salt and ground black pepper, to taste
- 40 g rocket, washed and dried

Preparation Instructions

1. Preheat the air fryer to 192°C.
2. Cover the air fryer basket with aluminium foil and grease lightly with oil. Put the figs in the air fryer basket and air fry for 10 minutes.
3. In a bowl, combine the chickpeas and cumin seeds.
4. Remove the air fried figs from the air fryer and replace with the chickpeas. Air fry for 10 minutes. Leave to cool.
5. In the meantime, prepare the dressing. Mix the balsamic vinegar, olive oil, salt and pepper.
6. In a salad bowl, combine the rocket with the cooled figs and chickpeas.
7. Toss with the sauce and serve.

Gorgonzola Mushrooms with Horseradish Mayo

Prep time: 15 minutes

Cook Time: 10 minutes

Serves 5

Ingredients

- 60 g bread crumbs
- 2 cloves garlic, pressed
- 2 tablespoons chopped fresh coriander
- ⅓ teaspoon coarse sea salt
- ½ teaspoon crushed red pepper flakes
- 1½ tablespoons olive oil
- 20 medium mushrooms, stems removed
- 55 g grated Gorgonzola cheese
- 55 g low-fat mayonnaise
- 1 teaspoon prepared horseradish, well-drained
- 1 tablespoon finely chopped fresh parsley

Preparation Instructions

1. Preheat the air fryer to 192°C.
2. Combine the bread crumbs together with the garlic, coriander, salt, red pepper, and olive oil.
3. Take equal-sized amounts of the bread crumb mixture and use them to stuff the mushroom caps. Add the grated Gorgonzola on top of each.
4. Put the mushrooms in a baking pan and transfer to the air fryer.
5. Air fry for 10 minutes, ensuring the stuffing is warm throughout.
6. In the meantime, prepare the horseradish mayo. Mix the mayonnaise, horseradish and parsley.
7. When the mushrooms are ready, serve with the mayo.

Air Fryer Crispy Tofu

Cooking Time: 20 minutes

Serves 4

Ingredients

- 400g firm tofu, drained and pressed
- 2 tbsp cornflour
- 1 tsp smoked paprika
- 1 tsp garlic powder

- 1/2 tsp salt
- 1/4 tsp black pepper
- Cooking spray

Preparation Instructions

1. Preheat the air fryer to 200°C.
2. Cut the tofu into small cubes.
3. In a small bowl, mix together the cornflour, smoked paprika, garlic powder, salt and black pepper.
4. Toss the tofu in the spice mixture until evenly coated.
5. Spray the air fryer basket with cooking spray.
6. Arrange the tofu in a single layer in the air fryer basket.
7. Cook for 10 minutes, then flip the tofu and cook for another 10 minutes until golden and crispy.
8. Serve hot with your favourite dipping sauce.

Nutrition Information (per serving): Calories: 114, Fat: 7g, Saturated Fat: 1g, Sodium: 334mg, Carbohydrates: 6g, Fibre: 1g, Sugar: 0g, Protein: 9g.

Baked Sweet Potato Falafel

Cook Time 25 minutes

Serves 4

Ingredients

- 400g canned chickpeas, drained and rinsed
- 400g sweet potato, peeled and grated
- 50g plain flour
- 1 small onion, chopped
- 2 garlic cloves, minced
- 1 tbsp ground cumin
- 1 tbsp ground coriander
- 1 tsp smoked paprika
- 1 tsp salt
- 2 tbsp olive oil

For the sauce:

- 150g Greek yoghurt
- 1 garlic clove, minced
- Juice of 1
- 2 lemon
- Salt and pepper to taste

Preparation Instructions

1. Preheat the air fryer to 180°C.
2. In a food processor, combine the chickpeas, grated sweet potato, plain flour, onion, garlic, cumin, coriander, paprika, and salt. Pulse until well combined.
3. Using your hands, shape the mixture into small balls.
4. Brush the falafel balls with olive oil.
5. Place the falafel balls in the air fryer basket and cook for 12-15 minutes, turning halfway through, until golden brown and crispy.
6. While the falafel cooks, mix together the Greek yoghurt, garlic, lemon juice, salt and pepper in a small bowl.
7. Serve the hot falafel with the sauce on the side.

Nutritional information per serving (including sauce):

Calories: 363, Fat: 13g, Saturated Fat: 2g, Sodium: 682mg, Carbohydrates: 51g, Fibre: 11g, Sugars: 8g, Protein: 14g.

Courgette Fritters

Cook Time 15 minutes

Serves 4

Ingredients

- 400g courgette, grated
- 100g crumbled feta cheese
- 50g plain flour
- 2 eggs, lightly beaten
- 2 tbsp chopped fresh parsley
- 1 garlic clove, minced
- Salt and pepper to taste
- 2 tbsp olive oil

Preparation Instructions

1. Preheat the air fryer to 180°C.
2. In a large bowl, combine the grated courgette, crumbled feta cheese, plain flour, beaten eggs, chopped parsley, minced garlic, salt, and pepper. Mix well.
3. Using your hands, shape the mixture into small patties.
4. Brush the patties with olive oil.
5. Place the patties in the air fryer basket and cook for 8-10 minutes, turning halfway through, until golden brown and crispy.
6. Serve the hot courgette fritters with a side salad or your favourite dipping sauce.

Nutritional information per serving:
Calories: 189 kcal Fat: 13g Carbohydrates: 10 g Fibre: 2g Protein: 8g

Garlic Cauliflower with Tahini

Prep time: 10 minutes

Cook Time: 20 minutes

Serves 4

Ingredients

Cauliflower:
- 500 g cauliflower florets (about 1 large head)
- 6 garlic cloves, smashed and cut into thirds
- 3 tablespoons vegetable oil
- ½ teaspoon ground cumin
- ½ teaspoon ground coriander
- ½ teaspoon coarse sea salt

Sauce:
- 2 tablespoons tahini (sesame paste)
- 2 tablespoons hot water
- 1 tablespoon fresh lemon juice
- 1 teaspoon minced garlic
- ½ teaspoon coarse sea salt

Preparation Instructions

1. For the cauliflower: In a large bowl, combine the cauliflower florets and garlic. Drizzle with the vegetable oil. Sprinkle the cumin, coriander, and salt. Toss until well coated.
2. Place the cauliflower in the air fryer basket. Set the air fryer to 200°C for 20 minutes, turning the cauliflower halfway through the Cooking Time.
3. Meanwhile, for the sauce: In a small bowl, combine the tahini, water, lemon juice, garlic, and salt. (The sauce will appear curdled at first, but keep stirring until you have a thick, creamy, smooth mixture.)
4. Transfer the cauliflower to a large serving bowl. Pour the sauce over and toss gently to coat. Serve immediately.

Green Tomato Salad

Prep time: 10 minutes

Cook Time: 8 to 10 minutes

Serves 4

Ingredients

- 4 green tomatoes
- ½ teaspoon salt
- 1 large egg, lightly beaten
- 50 g peanut flour
- 1 tablespoon Creole seasoning
- 1 (140 g) bag rocket
- **Buttermilk Dressing:**
- 230 g mayonnaise
- 120 g sour cream
- 2 teaspoons fresh lemon juice
- 2 tablespoons finely chopped fresh parsley
- 1 teaspoon dried dill
- 1 teaspoon dried chives
- ½ teaspoon salt
- ½ teaspoon garlic powder
- ½ teaspoon onion powder

Preparation Instructions

1. Preheat the air fryer to 200°C.
2. Slice the tomatoes into ½-inch slices and sprinkle with the salt. Let sit for 5 to 10 minutes.
3. Place the egg in a small shallow bowl. In another small shallow bowl, combine the peanut flour and Creole seasoning. Dip each tomato slice into the egg wash, then dip into the peanut flour mixture, turning to coat evenly.
4. Working in batches if necessary, arrange the tomato slices in a single layer in the air fryer basket and spray both sides lightly with olive oil. Air fry until browned and crisp, 8 to 10 minutes.
5. To make the buttermilk dressing: In a small bowl, whisk together the mayonnaise, sour cream, lemon juice, parsley, dill, chives, salt, garlic powder, and onion powder.
6. Serve the tomato slices on top of a bed of the rocket with the dressing on the side.

Caesar Whole Cauliflower

Prep time: 20 minutes

Cook Time: 30 minutes

Serves 2 to 4

Ingredients

• 3 tablespoons olive oil
• 2 tablespoons red wine vinegar
• 2 tablespoons Worcestershire sauce
• 2 tablespoons grated Parmesan cheese
• 1 tablespoon Dijon mustard
• 4 garlic cloves, minced
• 4 oil-packed anchovy fillets, drained and finely minced
• coarse sea salt and freshly ground black pepper, to taste
• 1 small head cauliflower (about 450 g), green leaves trimmed and stem trimmed flush • with the bottom of the head
• 1 tablespoon roughly chopped fresh flat-leaf parsley (optional)

Preparation Instructions

1. In a liquid measuring jug, whisk together the olive oil, vinegar, Worcestershire, Parmesan, mustard, garlic, anchovies, and salt and pepper to taste. Place the cauliflower head upside down on a cutting board and use a paring knife to make an "x" through the full length of the core. Transfer the cauliflower head to a large bowl and pour half the dressing over it. Turn the cauliflower head to coat it in the dressing, then let it rest, stem-side up, in the dressing for at least 10 minutes and up to 30 minutes to allow the dressing to seep into all its nooks and crannies.
2. Transfer the cauliflower head, stem-side down, to the air fryer and air fry at 170°C or 25 minutes. Drizzle the remaining dressing over the cauliflower and air fry at 200°C until the top of the cauliflower is golden brown and the core is tender, about 5 minutes more.
3. Remove the basket from the air fryer and transfer the cauliflower to a large plate. Sprinkle with the parsley, if you like, and serve hot.

Chapter 6   Snacks and Appetisers

Pickles Prepared in an Air Fryer

Prep time: 5 minutes

Cooking Time: 10 minutes

Serves: 4 people

Ingredients
- 16 pickle slices
- 60g all-purpose flour
- 1 teaspoon paprika
- 1/2 teaspoon garlic powder
- 1/4 teaspoon cayenne pepper
- 1 egg
- 60ml milk
- 60g panko bread crumbs
- Non-stick cooking spray

Preparation Instructions
1. Preheat the air fryer to 375°F (190°C).
2. In a small bowl, mix together the flour, paprika, garlic powder, and cayenne pepper.
3. In another bowl, whisk together the egg and milk.
4. Place the panko bread crumbs in a third bowl.
5. Dredge the pickle slices in the flour mixture, shaking off any excess. Dip them in the egg mixture, letting the excess drip off, and then coat them in the panko bread crumbs, pressing the crumbs onto the pickles to ensure they adhere.
6. Spray the air fryer basket with non-stick cooking spray.
7. Place the breaded pickles in the air fryer basket in a single layer, making sure they are not touching.
8. Cook for 8-10 minutes, or until golden brown and crispy.
9. Remove the pickles from the air fryer basket and serve immediately. Enjoy with your favourite dipping sauce!

Air Fryer Pork Chops

Prep time: 10 minutes

Cooking Time: 20 minutes

Serves: 2

Ingredients
- 2 bone-in pork chops (about 450g)
- 1 teaspoon paprika
- 1 teaspoon garlic powder
- 1 teaspoon onion powder
- 1 teaspoon dried thyme
- 1/2 teaspoon salt
- 1/4 teaspoon black pepper
- 1 tablespoon olive oil

Preparation Instructions
1. Preheat the air fryer to 380°F (190°C).
2. In a small bowl, mix together the paprika, garlic powder, onion powder, dried thyme, salt, and black pepper.
3. Rub the spice mixture onto the pork chops. Brush the pork chops with olive oil on both sides.
4. Place the pork chops in the air fryer basket in a single layer. Do not overcrowd the basket.
5. Cook the pork chops for 8-10 minutes on one side, then flip them over and cook for an additional 8-10 minutes, or until they reach an internal temperature of 145°F (63°C).
6. Remove the pork chops from the air fryer and let them rest for 5 minutes before serving.
7. Serve with your favorite sides, such as roasted vegetables or mashed potatoes. Enjoy!

Classic Jacket Potato (Beans & Cheese)

Prep time: 5 minutes

Cooking Time: 50 minutes

Serves: 4

Ingredients:

- 4 large potatoes
- 60g butter (4 tbsp)
- 1 tsp ground black pepper (optional)
- 1 tsp chilli flakes (optional)
- 500g baked beans
- 180g cheddar cheese

Preparation Instructions:

1. Preheat the air fryer at 180° for 5 minutes
2. Make multiple insertions in the potato with a fork, ensuring they do not burst whilst baking
3. Place the potatoes into the air fryer and select the 'bake roast' function at 200° for 50 minutes (if applicable)
4. Meanwhile, place the baked beans in the microwave or cooking pan for 2 minutes
5. Retrieve the potatoes and cut down the centre of the potatoes
6. Plate the potatoes up and layer a tbsp of butter in the centres
7. Divide the baked beans by 4 and dollop them in the centre of each potato
8. Top the hot baked beans with cheese, which should melt it partially
9. Season the potatoes with ground black pepper, chilli flakes (optional) and then serve

Bruschetta with Basil Pesto

Prep time: 10 minutes

Cooking Time: 5 to11 minutes

Serves: 4

Ingredients:

- 8 slices French bread, ½ inch thick
- 2 tablespoons softened butter
- 125 g shredded Mozzarella cheese
- 125 g basil pesto
- 125 g chopped grape tomatoes
- 2 spring onions, thinly sliced

Preparation Instructions:

1. Preheat the air fryer to 176ºC.
2. Spread the bread with the butter and place butter-side up in the air fryer basket. Bake for 3 to 5 minutes, or until the bread is light golden brown.
3. Remove the bread from the basket and top each piece with some of the cheese. Return to the basket in 2 batches and bake for 1 to 3 minutes, or until the cheese melts.
4. Meanwhile, combine the pesto, tomatoes, and spring onions in a small bowl.
5. When the cheese has melted, remove the bread from the air fryer and place on a serving plate. Top each slice with some of the pesto mixture and serve.

Black Bean Corn Dip

Prep time: 10 minutes

Cooking Time: 10 minutes

Serves: 4

Ingredients:

- ½ (425 g) can black beans, drained and rinsed
- ½ (425 g) can corn, drained and rinsed
- 60 ml chunky salsa
- 57 g low-fat soft white cheese
- 60 ml shredded low-fat Cheddar cheese
- ½ teaspoon ground cumin
- ½ teaspoon paprika
- Salt and freshly ground black pepper, to taste

Preparation Instructions:

1. Preheat the air fryer to 164°C.
2. In a medium bowl, mix together the black beans, corn, salsa, soft white cheese, Cheddar cheese, cumin, and paprika. Season with salt and pepper and stir until well combined.
3. Spoon the mixture into a baking dish.
4. Place baking dish in the air fryer basket and bake until heated through, about 10 minutes.
5. Serve hot.

Spicy Tortilla Chips

Prep time: 5 minutes

Cooking Time: 8 to 12 minutes

Serves: 4

Ingredients:

- ½ teaspoon ground cumin
- ½ teaspoon paprika
- ½ teaspoon chilli powder
- ½ teaspoon salt
- Pinch cayenne pepper
- 8 (6-inch) corn tortillas, each cut into 6 wedges
- Cooking spray

Preparation Instructions:

1. Preheat the air fryer to 192°C. Lightly spritz the air fryer basket with cooking spray.
2. Stir together the cumin, paprika, chilli powder, salt, and pepper in a small bowl.
3. Working in batches, arrange the tortilla wedges in the air fryer basket in a single layer. Lightly mist them with cooking spray. Sprinkle some seasoning mixture on top of the tortilla wedges.
4. Air fry for 4 to 6 minutes, shaking the basket halfway through, or until the chips are lightly browned and crunchy.
5. Repeat with the remaining tortilla wedges and seasoning mixture.
6. Let the tortilla chips cool for 5 minutes and serve.

Roasted Grape Dip

Prep time: 10 minutes

Cooking Time: 8 to12 minutes

Serves: 6

Ingredients:

- 475 ml seedless red grapes, rinsed and patted dry
- 1 tablespoon apple cider vinegar
- 1 tablespoon honey
- 240 ml low-fat Greek yoghurt
- 2 tablespoons semi-skimmed milk
- 2 tablespoons minced fresh basil

Preparation Instructions:

1. In the air fryer basket, sprinkle the grapes with the cider vinegar and drizzle with the honey. Toss to coat. Roast the grapes at 192°C for 8 to 12 minutes, or until shrivelled but still soft. Remove from the air fryer.
2. In a medium bowl, stir together the yoghurt and milk.
3. Gently blend in the grapes and basil. Serve immediately or cover and chill for 1 to 2 hours.

Calzone

Prep time: 10 minutes

Cooking Time: 10 to12 minutes

Serves: 2

Ingredients:

- 1 batch of homemade or ready-made whole wheat pizza dough
- 100g of low-Fat ricotta cheese
- 100g of turkey pepperoni or diced cooked chicken breast
- 100g of low Fat mozzarella cheese, shredded
- 2 tablespoons of olive oil
- 1 teaspoon of dried oregano
- 1/2 teaspoon of garlic powder
- Salt and pepper, to taste

Preparation Instructions:

1. Preheat the air fryer to 180°C.
2. Roll out the pizza dough into a large circle, about 12 cm thick.
3. In a mixing bowl, combine the ricotta cheese, pepperoni or cooked chicken, mozzarella cheese, dried oregano, garlic powder, salt, and pepper. Mix until well combined.
4. Spread the mixture over half of the rolled-out dough, leaving a 2.5 cm border around the edge.
5. Fold the other half of the dough over the filling and press the edges together to seal.
6. Brush the top of the calzone with olive oil.
7. Place the calzone in the air fryer and cook for 10-12 minutes or until the crust is golden brown and the filling is hot.

Old Bay Chicken Wings

Prep time: 10 minutes

Cooking Time: 12 to15 minutes

Serves: 4

Ingredients:

- 2 tablespoons Old Bay or all-purpose seasoning
- 2 teaspoons baking powder
- 2 teaspoons salt
- 900 g chicken wings, patted dry
- Cooking spray

Preparation Instructions:

1. Preheat the air fryer to 204°C. Lightly spray the air fryer basket with cooking spray.
2. Combine the seasoning, baking powder, and salt in a large zip-top plastic bag. Add the chicken wings, seal, and shake until the wings are thoroughly coated in the seasoning mixture.
3. Lay the chicken wings in the air fryer basket in a single layer and lightly mist with cooking spray. You may need to work in batches to avoid overcrowding.
4. Air fry for 12 to 15 minutes, flipping the wings halfway through, or until the wings are lightly browned and the internal temperature reaches at least 74°C on a meat thermometer.
5. Remove from the basket to a plate and repeat with the remaining chicken wings.
6. Serve hot.

Greek-style spanakopita

Serves: 4

Prep time: 30 minutes

Cooking Time: 20 minutes

Ingredients:

- 250g fresh spinach, washed and chopped
- 150g feta cheese, crumbled
- 1 onion, chopped
- 2 garlic cloves, minced
- 2 eggs
- 2 tbsp olive oil
- 1 tsp dried dill
- 1 tsp dried mint
- 1/4 tsp grated nutmeg
- Salt and black pepper, to taste
- 8 sheets filo pastry
- 60g butter, melted

Preparation Instructions:

1. Preheat the air fryer to 180°C.
2. In a pan over medium heat, add 1 tablespoon of olive oil and sauté the onion until translucent.
3. Add the minced garlic and sauté for another minute.
4. Add the chopped spinach and cook until wilted. Remove from heat and let it cool down.
5. In a bowl, beat the eggs and add crumbled feta cheese, dill, mint, nutmeg, salt, and pepper. Mix well.
6. Add the spinach mixture and stir until well combined.
7. Brush each sheet of filo pastry with melted butter and place them on top of each other.
8. Cut the stacked filo pastry sheets in half lengthwise to make two long strips.
9. Spoon the spinach mixture along the bottom edge of the filo pastry strip, leaving a 1cm border at the bottom and sides.
10. Fold the sides of the pastry over the filling and roll up the pastry tightly from the bottom to the top.
11. Brush the spanakopita with butter and place them in the air fryer basket. Cook for 20 minutes or until golden brown and crispy. Serve hot or at room temperature.

Shishito Peppers with Herb Dressing

Serves: 2-4

Prep time: 10 minutes
Cooking Time: 6 minutes

Ingredients:

- 170 g Shishito peppers
- 1 tablespoon vegetable oil
- Kosher or coarse sea salt and freshly ground black pepper, to taste
- 125 g mayonnaise
- 2 tablespoons finely chopped fresh basil leaves
- 2 tablespoons finely chopped fresh flat-leaf parsley
- 1 tablespoon finely chopped fresh tarragon
- 1 tablespoon finely chopped fresh chives
- Finely grated zest of ½ lemon
- 1 tablespoon fresh lemon juice
- Flaky sea salt, for serving

Preparation Instructions:

1. Preheat the air fryer to 204°C.
2. In a bowl, toss together the Shishitos and oil to evenly coat and season with kosher salt and black pepper. Transfer to the air fryer and air fry for 6 minutes, shaking the basket halfway through, or until the Shishitos are blistered and lightly charred.
3. Meanwhile, in a small bowl, whisk together the mayonnaise, basil, parsley, tarragon, chives, lemon zest, and lemon juice.
4. Pile the peppers on a plate, sprinkle with flaky sea salt, and serve hot with the dressing.

Air Fryer Hot Pickle Chips

Prep time: 10 minutes

Cooking Time: 10 minutes

Serves: 4

Ingredients:

- 240ml sliced pickles, drained
- 60g all-purpose flour
- 1 tsp smoked paprika
- ½ tsp garlic powder
- ½ tsp onion powder
- ¼ tsp cayenne pepper
- ¼ tsp salt
- ¼ tsp black pepper
- 120ml buttermilk
- 60g panko breadcrumbs
- Cooking spray

Preparation Instructions:

1. Preheat your air fryer to 200°C.
2. In a small bowl, mix together flour, smoked paprika, garlic powder, onion powder, cayenne pepper, salt, and black pepper.
3. Place buttermilk in a separate bowl and panko breadcrumbs in another bowl.
4. Dip pickle slices into the flour mixture, then into the buttermilk, and finally into the panko breadcrumbs, making sure they are coated evenly.
5. Place the coated pickle slices in the air fryer basket in a single layer.
6. Spray the pickle slices with cooking spray.
7. Cook for 10 minutes or until the pickle chips are golden brown and crispy, flipping them over halfway through the Cooking Time. Once the pickle chips are done, remove them from the air fryer and serve hot.

Crab Cakes

Prep time: 15 minutes

Cooking Time: 10 minutes

Serves: 4

Ingredients:

- 1 lb. (450g) crab meat, drained and picked over for shells
- 60g breadcrumbs
- 60g mayonnaise
- 1 large egg, beaten
- 2 tbsp Dijon mustard
- 1 tbsp Worcestershire sauce
- 10g chopped fresh parsley
- 10g chopped scallions
- 1 tsp Old Bay seasoning
- ¼ tsp salt
- ¼ tsp black pepper
- Cooking spray

Preparation Instructions:

1. Preheat your air fryer to 200°C.
2. In a large mixing bowl, combine the crab meat, breadcrumbs, mayonnaise, beaten egg, Dijon mustard, Worcestershire sauce, chopped parsley, chopped scallions, Old Bay seasoning, salt, and black pepper. Mix well until all Ingredients are combined.
3. Form the crab mixture into small patties, approximately 2-3 inches (5-7. 5cm) in diameter.
4. Lightly coat the air fryer basket with cooking spray.
5. Arrange the crab cakes in the air fryer basket in a single layer, leaving a little space between each one.
6. Cook for 10 minutes or until the crab cakes are golden brown and cooked through, flipping them over halfway through the Cooking Time. Once the crab cakes are done, remove them from the air fryer and serve immediately with your favorite dipping sauce

Kale Chips with Tex-Mex Dip

Prep time: 10 minutes

Cooking Time: 10 minutes

Serves: 4-6

Ingredients
- 1 large bunch of kale, washed and dried
- 1 tablespoon olive oil
- 1 teaspoon garlic powder
- 1 teaspoon chili powder
- 1/2 teaspoon cumin
- 1/4 teaspoon salt
- **For the dip:**
- 240ml plain Greek yogurt
- 1 tablespoon taco seasoning
- 1 teaspoon lime juice
- 15g chopped fresh cilantro

Preparation Instructions:
1. Preheat the air fryer to 350°F (180°C).
2. Remove the kale leaves from the thick stems and tear them into bite-sized pieces.
3. In a bowl, mix together the kale, olive oil, garlic powder, chili powder, cumin, and salt.
4. Place the kale in the air fryer basket in a single layer, making sure not to overcrowd the basket.
5. Cook the kale chips for 5-7 minutes, or until crisp and lightly browned.
6. While the kale chips are cooking, mix together the Greek yogurt, taco seasoning, lime juice, and cilantro in a small bowl.
7. Serve the kale chips hot out of the air fryer with the Tex-Mex dip on the side.

Thai-style shrimp cakes

Serves: 4

Prep time: 15 minutes

Cook Time: 12 minutes

Ingredients:
- 300g raw shrimp, peeled and deveined
- 40g chopped fresh coriander
- 45g chopped spring onions
- 2 cloves garlic, minced
- 1 red chilli, seeded and minced
- 1 tbsp fish sauce
- 1 tbsp red curry paste
- 1 egg
- 60g breadcrumbs
- 1 tbsp vegetable oil

Instructions:
1. In a food processor, pulse the shrimp until finely minced.
2. Add coriander, spring onions, garlic, chilli, fish sauce, red curry paste, and egg.
3. Pulse until everything is well combined.
4. Transfer the mixture to a bowl, and add the breadcrumbs.
5. Mix until well combined.
6. Using wet hands, shape the mixture into small cakes and place them on a plate.
7. Preheat the air fryer to 200°C.
8. Brush the shrimp cakes with oil, and place them in the air fryer basket in a single layer.
9. Select air fry at 200°C for 12 minutes.
10. Flip the cakes halfway through the Cooking Time using silicone-tipped tongs to ensure even cooking.
11. Once cooked, remove the cakes from the air fryer and serve hot with your favourite dipping sauce. Enjoy!

Jalapeño Poppers filled with soft white cheese

Prep time: 10 minutes

Cooking Time: 10 minutes

Serves: 4-6

Ingredients

- 12 fresh jalapeño peppers
- 110g soft white cheese, like cream cheese or goat cheese
- 30g breadcrumbs
- 1/4 tsp garlic powder
- Salt and pepper, to taste
- 2 eggs, beaten
- 30g all-purpose flour

Preparation Instructions:

1. Preheat the air fryer to 375°F (190°C).
2. Wash and dry the jalapeño peppers. Cut them in half lengthwise and remove the seeds and membranes using a spoon.
3. In a mixing bowl, combine the soft white cheese, breadcrumbs, garlic powder, salt, and pepper. Mix well to create a smooth paste.
4. Using a spoon, fill each jalapeño half with the cheese mixture.
5. Place the beaten eggs in a shallow dish and the all-purpose flour in another shallow dish.
6. Dip each stuffed jalapeño half in the flour and shake off the excess. Then, dip it in the beaten eggs and coat well.
7. Place the coated jalapeño halves in the air fryer basket, making sure they are not touching.
8. Cook the jalapeño poppers in the air fryer for 10 minutes, or until golden brown and crisp. You may need to flip them halfway through cooking to ensure even browning.
9. Remove the jalapeño poppers from the air fryer and let them cool for a few minutes before serving. Enjoy!

Printed in Great Britain
by Amazon

22010014R00044